THE SIN OF RACISM

How to be Set Free

Selena Johnson

Hamilton Books
A member of
The Rowman & Littlefield Publishing Group
Lanham · Boulder · New York · Toronto · Oxford

Copyright © 2006 by
Hamilton Books
4501 Forbes Boulevard
Suite 200
Lanham, Maryland 20706
Hamilton Books Acquisitions Department (301) 459-3366

PO Box 317
Oxford
OX2 9RU, UK

Library of Congress Control Number: 2006923889
ISBN-13: 978-0-7618-3509-7 (paperback : alk. paper)
ISBN-10: 0-7618-3509-1 (paperback : alk. paper)

CONTENTS

Author Biographical Sketch

ILLUSTRATIONS

Preface

The purpose of this book is to enlighten readers to racism as a sin. It will help those who reject Christ for reasons based on race to overcome so they can receive the gift of salvation through the Lord Jesus Christ. It is also for those who are already saved but they still struggle with this dilemma. They can restore right relationship to Him by acknowledging and overcoming this transgression. It is a highly evangelistic tool to equip those interested or called to spiritual battle within the realm of racism and to minister to those seekers who have serious concerns and misconceptions about racism and the Christian church. There are many books today that deal with the multi-cultural aspect of Christianity as well as many that point out the evils of racism as it relates to our faith. However, there are none like this book that delve into the sordid past of American racism with candid truth as well as look to the future with the hope of today's changing society.

I am compelled here to relate my personal testimony, how I came to know the saving grace of the Lord Jesus Christ. Now when I was a child, my mother was adamant that my sister and I should get into the church because she came from a very religious family. Many reverends, deacons and loyal workers were

among her fifteen siblings and our other relatives. And so when I
was fourteen years of age I joined the church. I walked the aisle
for myself. They probably had me to repeat a prayer. The Reverend baptized me in the name of the Father, Son, and Holy Ghost.
He dunked me into the water as a sinner. I came up out of the
water—*a soaking-wet sinner!* There was no change within my
heart. I attended church regularly, joined the choir, and partici-
pated in a few youth activities.

After moving from home for college I fell out of going to
church. Many years later when I moved to New York City, I felt
the need to go back to church. However, it was only to relieve
the pressure of my stressful life. Anyone who has ever lived in
New York City knows how fast paced it is and also how callous
people, myself included, can be in their haste. There is also a
great deal of racial tension, crime, and homelessness. Living in
New York made me keenly aware that there is an evil force in
the world. I desperately wanted protection from that force. I
would go to church to weep and moan and feel comforted, but I
had no understanding of the true meaning of Christianity because
I was completely focused on myself. I was involved in black ac-
tivist groups and protests that many would categorize as radical.
I collected articles about racial incidences and protests in other
places, savoring the reading and re-reading of every word. I
would constantly review and ponder these things to feed my anger about racism. I was the epitome of woe. In church I wal-
lowed in my own sorrow and anger thinking that the God would
see my great suffering and anxiety and because of it would deem
me worthy to go to heaven.

After leaving New York City, I wound up in the Baltimore
area of Maryland. Anger about racism had become my religion. I
did not bother to find a new church home. "The Movement" (for
black people to get justice in this country) was my god. My salvation, I thought, would be to do something great for the movement. I was ready even to die for this cause. One day, I came to
realize that fighting racism was a wrong religion. It was not that
it is not a worthy cause, because it is. But it was too heavy a burden for my soul.

This revelation came to me upon watching the movie *Rose-wood* (directed by John Singleton, released around 1998). The movie is about a town of black people who prospered during the Reconstruction era. Surrounding whites got jealous, then terrorized and ultimately burned the town down, killing and maiming as they went. The climax of the movie comes when the main character, a very large, stocky black man is taken by a white lynch mob. They try to hang him, but they do not succeed. He is so strong he breaks the noose with his neck muscles and frees himself! The white men run away terrified. He chases one of them down and has him cornered. The drama and suspense reach a crescendo as you wait to see if he will get revenge and kill him, or let him go. I screamed at my television "KILL HIM! KILL HIM! Kiiiiiilllllllll HIMMMM!

All of my pent up anger and anguish came out. I wept bitterly. Then I wept sadly. I was saddened to realize the weight of malice that was in my heart toward white people. I wanted to kill them. I had a murderous heart. But I was confused, too—because I did not honestly want to kill all white people. What about the people who had helped me, who mentored me, supported me, befriended me? I realized it was all too heavy for me. Only someone bigger than all of it, outside of all of it, someone just and unbiased could solve the problem. Only God was big enough to handle this issue. Racism was too heavy for my one small human soul. And, unbeknownst to me at that time, it was distracting me from coming to Christ. I was weary that day, alone in my apartment with my angry, murderous heart and my television. That day I decided to go back to church to try to find the solution outside of this world. I did not come to faith in Christ right away, but eventually He drew me in.

I began attending Bethel AME church in Baltimore. There, I was challenged in my faith by the very Spirit-filled services and all the talk about salvation through Christ. One associate minister, Rev. David Deveaux, used to always say before the altar call, "If you are not sure whether or not you are saved, you are NOT saved." And the leader of the house, Dr. Frank Madison Reid III many times said something like, "If Jesus were to walk in that

door right now to claim His own, would you be absolutely sure
that He would take you? Do you know that you know that you
know that you know?!!!" When I heard these things, I would try
to rationalize intellectually that I was basically a good person, so
why would Jesus not take me? I did not yet understand that, although God's Spirit was drawing me, that I had not truly received Christ Jesus. But I did enjoy the lively praise at Bethel
and in turn was heavily into black gospel music. One of my favorite artists is Kirk Franklin, who is somewhat controversial
because he uses a hip-hop sound in his music. I marveled at the
passion for God that I heard in his voice and in his songs. My
soul began to wonder how he came to feel so strongly.

That summer some of my close relatives were reading the
Left Behind series of books by Tim Lahaye and Jerry Jenkins.
These books are very popular end times dramatizations based on
the book of Revelation, the last book in the Bible. I consider
them historical fiction because I believe God's word is true.
Therefore parts of the book of Revelation are history foretold.
Anyway, my family was quite enthralled in their readings and
recommended highly that I try them. I thought they might be
entertaining books, but I was sure that the authors, two white
men, were probably conservative Republicans, and could not
possibly give me any insight into God. As it turns out, their
writings actually demonstrate, through fictional characters, how
a person truly is saved by earnestly praying the prayer of salvation to the Lord, Jesus Christ. About one third of the way
through book number three I realized that, in contrast to these
characters, I was not really saved!

This revelation came to me on a Thursday. That Sunday
when I went to church my heart was heavy with the clear understanding that I had been phony with the Lord for close to twenty
years. I thank God that Bethel is a praying church and that we
were always encouraged to pray out loud during service. When
the time came for the congregation to pray, I prayed aloud to
Jesus to forgive me of my sins. I told him I realized who He is
and that He paid the price for me when He hung on the cross. I
thanked Him for taking the punishment for me for all of my sins,
but especially for the way I had treated my mother when she was

ill with terminal cancer. I thought this transgression even Jesus would not pardon. There are no words I can write here to explain the relief, joy, and peace that came over me that moment Jesus forgave me and took me in. Jesus confirmed with me that I was His and He was mine and that I was saved! If you have not done this for yourself, I cannot urge you enough to repent and receive Christ as your Lord and Savior.

One note of clarification; I do acknowledge that there are many forms of racism in the world besides the black/white racism in America. Conflicts have arisen and discriminatory practices have been perpetrated against others besides the descendants of slavery in America. This book, however, does not deal with the panoply of cultural differences in the world, but instead focuses on the specific strain between blacks and whites in America. Why? I focus on this particular conflict for many reasons. The duration of this confusion is quite remarkable in that the problem is centuries old. There are also so very many other ills, or spin-off sins as I call them, that have flourished because of this original ugly crime. Moreover, there seems to be a hopeless resignation regarding racism as though it is insurmountable, endless, and eternal. This mindset is decidedly unbiblical. The Bible teaches us that nothing is impossible with God (Luke 1:37, Genesis 18:14). Of course sin will not be abolished from the earth until God removes it. There will always be murderers, adulterers, thieves and yes people who hate and oppress others. However, the pain and suffering, the tension, anger, fear, poverty, and aberrancies being experienced in black America today as the direct result of the heritage of slavery, the sin of racism, can be overcome.

This sin has permeated not only America's consciousness in a widespread way, but it has also had far-reaching affects worldwide. I have a passion for tackling this issue because I am an African American and therefore it has affected my life greatly. It was my obsession before I got saved. Even after Jesus came into my life, I still had racial rage and difficulties and would often record these in my prayer journal. Those writings along with the research that ensued have resulted in this book.

Racism has been a personal hindrance to me in 1) finally accepting Jesus Christ as Lord of my life as well as 2) witnessing to white people 3) being on one accord with my white brothers and sisters in Christ 4) forgiving and leaving this pain at the altar, and 5) staying in right relationship to God, especially regarding current events. I want to share the conclusions that the Lord has shown me and testify about how He has helped me down the path to healing from this sin. My earnest prayer is that God, according to His holy and perfect will, will use this book to break the chains that racism has on the hearts, souls, and minds of many in this nation, and even worldwide that they might not have to struggle as I did.

First and foremost I give honor to God for loving me enough to change me. I thank Him for inspiring me and empowering me to write on this difficult subject. I also want to thank my husband, Paul, for his love, patience, support, and his reviews of my preliminary writing. Thanks also go to my sister, Lisa, my brother-in-law, Jay, and their family for allowing me time to write while I lived with them. I am grateful also to the people who proofread my first draft, Aunt Juanita, Kim, and Dr. Leonard Wheeler. I also thank my church families and the United Methodist Church for their love and support.

Introduction

Before I became a Christian, whenever I did something wrong, in other words whenever I committed a sin, I would rationalize in my own mind why the thing was justifiable. I would blame someone, something, or some circumstance. I reasoned also that the transgression was balanced out by the fact I was basically a good person. Rarely did I repent and ask for forgiveness. Even if I did, I asked it of the person whom I had wronged and not of God. However, whether I apologized or not, I could never quite rid myself of the guilt of that thing—whatever it was. I would have to leave a job, a situation, or a relationship to ease my mind. Sometimes I would vilify that person or persons against whom I had transgressed. Or I would try to show them that I was really a good person by being as perfect as I could. Then maybe they would see that I could not possibly be wrong, so it must be they. Nevertheless, the thing would continue to fester, even if it lay dormant for long periods of time. This is what I call un-repented sin. It is a spot on your soul that keeps nagging you no matter what you do. Some of these spots are bigger and more malignant than others. We all have them. There are no exceptions regardless of how well thought out one's rationale may be.

Let me relate a personal experience as an example of un-repented sin. When I was in high school my mother was diagnosed with cancer. She lived with the illness for four years. Towards the end of her life she suffered greatly. However, my main focus during all of her trials and grief was on me, myself, and I. Outwardly I appeared to be a good person. I graduated valedictorian of my class and went on to attend the prestigious Massachusetts Institute of Technology. But on the inside I was ashamed of my mother for being sickly and frail. I was also angry with her for not being there for me during those years of transition. I was so self-centered that I did not even cry at her funeral! I was determined not to let all the people, who I perceived as gawking, see me weak and humbled. I had not shown her very much compassion during her illness and I was determined to keep my stance.

The price, however, for trying to cover this un-repented sin was high. I had to convince myself that my career, my education, and my mind were so very important that it was worth dishonoring my mother and not showing her the love I should have while she yet lived. So—I worked harder and harder every day. I studied more and more. Every minute that I was not working towards a goal, I felt guilty. I showed great bitterness and anger towards anyone who tried to hinder or discourage me. In my subconscious, insecurity and doubt reigned. Was this transgression really worth all of the energy of trying to cover it up and justify it? It was not until I trusted in Christ to relieve me of the transgression that I could find any peace.

What does this have to do with the subject at hand, racism? In the same way that an individual cannot be made whole until he or she admits their guilt to Christ and becomes saved, this nation cannot truly be united until this sin, racism, is confronted and repented of. If I might be so bold as to compare this nation to myself, America is not so important or such a good country as to have this terrible blot be outweighed by her good deeds. Neither can she blame black people, the victims, for this problem. Racism weighs heavily on her conscious like my guilt about my mother and my other sins did. The guilt grows like a malignancy while this country tries to ignore it. It stirs up bitterness and anger whenever she is confronted with or hindered by this issue. To begin the journey toward racial healing, we first need to understand the basic concepts of sin and salvation. Then we must admit that racism is in fact a sin and face the ugly truth. How did it happen? Why did it happen? What are its effects? How can we be rid of racism?

Note: There are many references to Biblical passages in this book. Unless otherwise noted, the King James Version is being used. Refer to the diagram below for explanation.

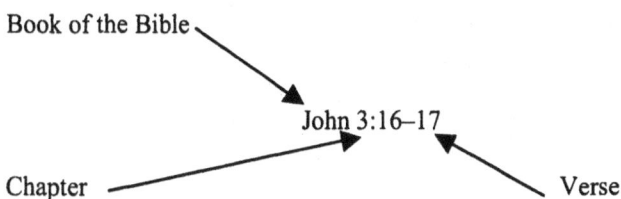

Book of the Bible

John 3:16–17

Chapter

Verse

Chapter One

The Sin of Racism

What is sin exactly? Sin is anything that goes against God's will. It is anything that conflicts with His Word. When God made Adam and Eve, they were sinless. Because of the original sin they committed by disobeying God, we are all born in sin, all sinners in need of salvation. What is the weight of this sin, racism? Sin is sin is sin, right? And God hates sin. ALL sin. But some sins are weightier than others. This particular sin, racism, because it has been able to manifest itself worldwide and in a variety of ways and for such a long duration—must be examined specially.

The dictionary defines racism as "a belief that race is the primary determinant of human traits and capacities and that racial differences produce an inherent superiority of a particular race. [It is] racial prejudice or discrimination."[1] The particular incident of racism referred to in this book is the belief that people of African descent in the United States, especially those descendants of slaves, are inherently inferior. Herein I am referring to the racism that is defined by discrimination and prejudices of white Americans against black Americans and vice versa.

Racism, therefore, is a sin because it goes against God's will that we love our neighbors as ourselves. It goes against His word, the Bible, which tells us that we, as human beings, were all created in His image. We all descended from the mother of all mankind, Eve, as opposed to from apes, who evolved from amoeba. Racism is a sin—one inspired by Satan, the father of lies. He has many people bound by confusion surrounding this issue. When people's hearts, minds, and souls are focused on the anger, hatred, fear, guilt, shame, and pain of racism or on a false sense of superiority it distracts us from seeing the beauty of Jesus Christ. On an individual level this sin that originated in the African slave trade has, I suspect, hindered many from receiving Jesus as their personal Savior. It also is an obstacle to many of us already in Christ because we have not been able to restore right relationship to God concerning this touchy subject. It thereby also hinders the body of Christ from behaving as we ought—as one.

Racism is a corporate sin. A group of people, as opposed to an individual, perpetrated it. Racism has its roots in slavery. Slavery was an institution sanctioned and imposed by the government of the United States. Many people in this country benefited and even still today stand on the foundation built by the economic security that slavery created.

Racism is un-repented corporate sin. In other words, Jesus paid the penalty for this sin, but the offending group has not asked Him for forgiveness. Individuals may have asked and received the mercy of His forgiveness, but as a whole, this nation and the world have not. Therefore, this un-repented, corporate sin weighs on us particularly in America in a way that casts a shadow over much of the good we attempt to do. Because we have not been purged of this sin, it does not matter how long ago slavery occurred. Its stench lingers on. I label it an iniquity because it has had such a long endurance and a "creep power" so to speak.

We need to be freed from racism, from the un-repented corporate sin of racism. Why, because it will continue to grow and fester if it is not dealt with. Sooner or later it will consume us. Racism began with the mid-Atlantic slave trade, but it escalated with the pseudo-scientific racism of the early 20th century and then the overt segregation and discrimination of the Jim Crow era. It continues with the covert racism of today. Satan has pricked men's pride and exacted a high yield for his evil goals through the sin of racism. The devil is our enemy. Our goal is to beat him. Both black and white people are guilty of letting racism flourish and thus both blacks and whites suffer under this burden. Therefore, I sincerely believe that both groups would benefit if we can be rid of this particular yoke that Satan has on us.

How can we be set free? Plainly said racism can only be overcome through the sin bearer Jesus Christ. He is the only one who can free us of this devilish bondage. He can free us individually and corporately. We must admit to Him that we are guilty of this sin, believing sincerely that He can cleanse us. We must forgive each other as He has forgiven us. Then we can do whatever else the Holy Spirit guides us to do for reparations.

Salvation is being freed from sin. For individuals, the only way to be saved is by receiving Jesus Christ as Lord and Savior of your life. Salvation is confessing with your mouth and believing with all your heart that Jesus Christ atoned for all of your sins on the cross and in His resurrection from the dead. (Romans 10:9). We can only be saved by God's grace through faith in Christ and not by any good deeds of our own. (Ephesians 2:8–9). If you are someone who feels the call of salvation on your life, but has not yet prayed and received Christ, again I urge you to take this important step in your life. If the confusion and pain of racism has hindered you, do not allow it to any longer. Pray sincerely and ask Jesus to forgive you of ALL your sins, not just racism. Ask Him to be your Lord and Savior.

Chapter One Endnotes

1. Merriam-Webster Inc., Merriam-Webster Online Dictionary, www.m-w.com (Springfield, MA: Merriam-Webster Inc., 2005).

Chapter Two

Time Does NOT Heal All Wounds

Is this issue still relevant today? After all, slavery ended a hundred years ago. The slaves were freed. Does that not count for payment for the sin of slavery? Civil Rights and voting rights were bestowed to the descendents of slaves, and now there is a black middle class, many prominent blacks, and even black millionaires and billionaires. Nonetheless, this issue is very real and very critical. Racial overtones color almost every national issue. Explosive racial incidents crop up unexpectedly. A disproportionate percentage of the black population still lives below the poverty level in America. Racism has impacted even our land use (or what might more rightly be described as misuse). Also, many social ills of today are the rotten fruit of what was sown in racial sin many years ago. There is a direct connection from slavery to today's issues. The incidents and periods can be thought of like a connect-the-dots puzzle. The weightiness of this sin has caused it to have a tremendous ripple effect through time and lives. The impact of four hundred plus years of chattel slavery cannot be dismissed cavalierly. Its severity will not allow.

What are some examples of racial tensions overshadowing America? Recall the incidences of November 2000. The United States presidential election had come down to such a close call that the electoral votes in the state of Florida would be the deciding factor. The ballots were counted and recounted. The country anticipated the final outcome with bated breath. The two camps were waiting on pins and needles. Then, as is usual in times of adversity in this country, the beast of racism reared its ugly head. Why were the voting apparatus for the black neighborhoods in the Florida district under question antiquated and unreliable? Why were voters asked to show identification at polling sites in black neighborhoods? This is completely illegal. Why was there a police presence at many polling places in black neighborhoods? The presidency was stained. Many disenfranchised Americans felt the declared winner, though he legally took office, was not their president.

Another example is the aftermath of the September 11th terrorist attacks on the United States. Arab radicals hijacked four planes, flying two into the World Trade Center Towers in New York City. Another they flew into the Pentagon and yet another crashed in Pennsylvania. Its target remains unknown. Because there is unity in persecution, American patriotism was running high in the days and months following these attacks. However, because racism still thrives here, many black people could only participate with a half-hearted wariness akin to an abused child enjoying a family outing. Then when Arab Americans complained of racial profiling as the authorities searched for suspects, we were compelled to point out that we have been profiled, pulled over in our cars, wrongly accused, and even executed on the spot for years and years. It is, in fact, nothing new.

Who will suffer most in a down economy? Who will benefit most from a strong economy? Why is it so noteworthy that Condoleezza Rice, the U.S. Secretary of State, is a black woman? If Colin Powell, the former U.S. Secretary of State, were white, would he not have been the obvious successor to the presidency for 2000? On and on the questions go?

And these are just the overtones and innuendos. What about when explosive flashpoints reveal the full prejudices of the American people in raw and unexpected ways? In 1991 there was the Rodney King incident. I turned on my television and saw four white policemen brutally beating Rodney King, a black man, while he was handcuffed, chained, and lying on the ground. Every angry emotion I had ever had towards white people welled up inside of me afresh. Every insult and discrimination was revived as though it had just happened that day. For many black Americans this was proof positive of the epidemic of police brutality we had been complaining about for years, especially since the early 1980's when the Reagan/Bush era began. Conversely, many white Americans viewed this beating as an isolated, unfortunate incident. These two perspectives are completely at odds and thus tensions began. The tensions escalated to riots and rose to pandemonium when those same officers were acquitted of wrongdoing by an all-white jury in Semi Valley, California.

Another example is the trial of O. J. Simpson. Here was a famous black athlete on trial for the brutal murder of his white ex-wife. Why did people in this country follow this trial with such an intense interest, tuning in to watch on TV. day after day, making it the focus of much conversation of the day? What were white people's expectations? Did O.J. Simpson represent all of their fears of angry, murderous black men? Were they hoping for a modern-day lynching? Why were black students at Howard University cheering when the not guilty verdict came down? Were they happy that people had been brutally murdered? Or were they happy that the lynch mob was left unsatisfied? Were they happy that a tainted justice system taints all and not just some? True and raw feelings were revealed in the wake of this trial and shattered the fantasy images of racial harmony we get on America on T.V. An unhealthy uneasiness arose that permeated every office environment and cultural exchange. Even years later this subject can re-ignite sparks and ill feelings.

These are just a few examples. Even if it were proven beyond any shadow of a doubt that O.J. did or did not commit these murders, the underlying problem would still be unresolved. These questions would still linger. Another issue would arise in which racism's monstrous face could be clearly seen. Even theatrical accounts of past racial injustices, such as the movies *Roots* and *Rosewood*, can spark new flames. Navigating any national

issue or crisis is like walking through a minefield dotted with
hidden racial explosives.

Another result of racism is land abuse. The American city
has been relabeled as the "inner city." With that name come
many negative connotations. We think of poverty, run-down
buildings and roads, drugs, crime and, whether we dare to admit
it or not, black people. Surveys have found that people in America are not so much afraid of being poor as of being victims of
crime. The specter of angry, poor black people seeking revenge
for America's racism, looms large in the minds of many white
people. This fear has prompted them to move first to the out-
skirts of the city, and then further and further out as affluent
blacks follow them out into each successive ring. This has turned
large portions of our cities into urban wastelands. Municipalities
are left without a good tax base, which in turn exacerbates the
impoverished state. Coupled with that is the waste associated
with suburban sprawl. As people repeatedly abandon developed
areas for new virgin soil, natural resources are squandered. More
human effort is required to build infrastructure and support as
well.

> Even as I have seen, they that plow iniquity, and sow wicked-
> ness, reap the same, (Job 4:8)

As I already mentioned, the iniquities of slavery have left us
with certain wicked crops. These I call spin-off sins. They are
indicators of the weightiness of this sin. Some may question the
Biblical basis for rating sin because the Bible teaches us that
God hates sin—all sin. However, understanding the principal of
sowing what you reap clears that up. As the above quote from
the book of Job indicates, bad crops are as plentiful as the
amount of bad seed planted. If you sow iniquity and wickedness,
you reap *the same*—both in content and quantity. The Bible tells
us to "give, and it shall be given unto you; good measure,
pressed down, and shaken together, and running over, shall men
give into your bosom. For with the same measure that ye mete
withal it shall be measured to you again." (Luke 6:38) "He which
soweth sparingly shall reap also sparingly; and he which soweth

bountifully shall reap also bountifully." (II Corinthians 9:6) These scriptures apply to both the positive and negative seeds we sow.

The legacy of the sin of slavery is physical abuse, murder, rape, kidnappings, sexual promiscuity, profanity, drunkenness, reveling, dishonor to mothers and fathers, and child abuse. The murder rate among blacks, as well as other black-on-black crime statistics, is inordinately high. Africans were kidnapped from their homes and communities and sold to European slavers in vast numbers. Now we have a whole television series dedicated to missing persons. Every week I receive at least one flyer in the mail with one or more pictures of missing children on it. Across the top it reads, "Have You Seen Me?" Slavery was riddled with whippings and a variety of other humiliating tortures designed to keep the slave in fear and submission. Now we have spousal abuse, child abuse, fighting and murder in schools, and disgruntled employees killing their coworkers. Watch any television or movie drama and you will be bombarded with multiple images of violence and gore. Some would argue that there is no connection between the fictional violence we consume so avidly and the fact that this nation leads the world in crime, violence, and incarceration. I disagree. It is the fruit of the bad crop.

This passion for violence is particularly related to the gun. Guns are glorified as symbols of power and strength. The world, and this nation in particular, has a sick fascination with firepower. There is evidence that guns did play a certain role in the enslavement of Africans.[1] Guns were also a critical factor in keeping slaves in bondage and in European Americans taking territory from the indigenous people of America. Today we have out-of-control gun violence in the United States. America's great obsession with the gun has turned into a love/hate relationship. No one wants to be the victim of gun violence; therefore, many buy guns to protect themselves. The legislative battle rages over gun control. The old adage, live by the sword, die by the sword is certainly applicable here. It is also confirmed in scripture:

Then said Jesus unto him, Put up again thy sword into his
place: for all they that take the sword shall perish with the
sword. (Matthew 26:52)

The only relief slaves had from the monotony and drudgery
of grueling work was sexual release and alcohol. Because the
value of the slave who reproduced was high, sexual promiscuity
was certainly not discouraged by slave owners. In fact slave
women were ostensibly forced to have sexual relations with
slave owners as is evidenced by the many shades of African
American descendents of slavery today. Now our nation is virtually obsessed with sexual gratification. Pornography use has
risen dramatically and continues to be on the rise. Music and
music videos highlight and glorify promiscuity. The same dra-
mas that are infused with violence are typically interwoven with
sex scenes as well. Even situation comedy is largely reliant on
sexual innuendos as punch lines. The statistics on rape in this
country are astronomical and unprecedented. In the year 2000
alone there were an estimated 147,160 cases of rape/attempted
rape.[2] That figure only includes the *reported* cases. This is the
seed of slave ship rape and the violation of enslaved women re-
turning to haunt us. How many children in the United States are
sexually abused—by parents, day care providers, relatives,
teachers, even priests? Recent statistics say that 34% of sexual
assault victims are under the age of 12 years old. Another 33% is
between ages 12 and 17.[3] That would have been close to 99,000
cases, *reported* cases, in the year 2000. Even if this has not impacted every American family directly, there certainly have been
enough highly publicized incidences to foster an atmosphere of
anxiety and mistrust.

Alcohol consumption is another out-of-control ill. It is
widely accepted as one of the great pleasures of life, a reward for
a hard day's work. It has become the main attraction at most
secular celebrations. Alcohol as well as other forms of drugs are
glamorized and advertised as an anesthetic to the pain of life's
drudgery. Partying on the weekends has become the only thing
many people look forward to help them get through the stress of

the workweek. It is no coincidence that this is the same antidote slaves relied on.

Slavery also promoted the destruction of the family structure. Men were not authorities in their household because they could not be looked to for provision and protection. Women were disrespected as workhorses and with sexual abuse. These things taught children of slaves to have no respect for authority at home. The offshoot of that is disrespect for authority in general. It is no accident that rebellion fills the hearts of today's youth. Authority is seen as the enemy. During slavery, families were often sold from one another. Therefore, the children of slavery had no strong foundation in the family. Now we have a divorce rate of 70%. We have an inordinate number of split families, single-parent families, blended families, foster children and children awaiting adoption. The psychological and social damage to children is just now coming to light in adult children of divorce and broken homes.

Those who believe racism no longer exists would say that the problems of today are unrelated incidences and coincidences in relation to slavery. They would argue that it is far fetched to try to make this connection over such a large time span. It is not something that can be proven by empirical data. But if God's word is taken seriously and literally then it is certain that the bad crop is coming after the bad seed—even if it takes a while to arrive. These spin-off sins have sprung from the seed of slavery to swallow us like a Venus flytrap does to a fly.

Why then are the oppressed, the ones who did not sow the seeds, disproportionately affected, then? One might ask God if this is fair. I cannot fully understand or claim to be able to answer this question. I do know that Satan roams the earth seeking whom he may devour. The person's race is not his concern. It is their mind he is seeking to corrupt and their soul he wants to control. Perhaps we [black people] have taken this so much to heart that it is easier for the crop to grow in the turmoil-laden soil of our hearts. Un-forgiveness is a spiritual killer. We will delve deeper into forgiveness issues in the last chapter. Perhaps also the crop has taken hold in mainstream America in more subtle ways. Then again, it could be that many transgressors have earnestly repented individually, prayed for forgiveness, and God has granted pardon. There does not seem to be much fruit bearing evidence of that, however. I cannot really say what the answer is to this perplexing question. But I do know for certain that God is just. He is perfect. He is perfectly holy. Therefore, His judgments are right.

The most egregious result of slavery, however, far outweighs any and all of those already mentioned—*combined*. In many cases, the anger, shame, blame, guilt, and obsessions associated with slavery and racism have distracted people from their salvation in Christ Jesus. This most important spiritual battle will be explored in depth in later chapters. The results of continuing to ignore racism are astronomical. Conversely, to overcome this problem would mean tremendous rewards and bring thoroughly worthwhile benefits.

How did we get into this mess?!!! Exploring the bad seeds in more depth, it is critical to establish the relationship between the crop (racism), which did spring from the seed and the root (slavery). Why continue to hearken back to this ugly incident? It makes people uncomfortable and anxious. The reason is simple. It is because people cannot be a-historical. History affects people. That is why we study the past. Every nation and culture in the world studies its own history as well as the history of others. Now we even have the History Channel here in America. Its popularity seems a paradox with the unwillingness of students to learn history while in school. But because it is well presented and enticing, the History Channel has become wildly popular in a relatively short time.

Four hundred years of chattel slavery is a monumental occurrence in the African, American, and world history. It has an impact on us today just like other historical periods and events. Examine for example the American Revolution and how it affects Americans today. In this country we celebrate the fourth of July every year to commemorate the victory of this war, even though it happened over two hundred years ago. Imagine if someone suggested to America that we should just get over it. What if they said to stop wasting so much time, money and energy on flags, fireworks, and parades every year because that event is ancient history? Would not the outcry in this country be tremendous? Would not that person be rejected and rebuked? Well it is just as ludicrous to declare that black Americans should forget our history. We can not simply forget about four hundred years of slavery because it impacts our lives heavily today.

Time does NOT heal all wounds. Even if it did, we still could not apply that balm to racial hatred because there has been no period of healing. There has been a continuum of prejudices in different forms, which have caused the sore of racism not only to have its scab picked raw, but the wound actually re-injured. In spiritual terms, Satan has gone unchecked here and therefore has escalated his attack and advanced.[4] Some of the re-injury is obvious and blatant, like the rise of the Klu Klux Klan. Some is more subtle like unemployment, disenfranchisement, and economic disparity. This is a generational curse, because unfortunately the legacy of slavery has been inherited by each new generation. Generational fear, generational anger, and generational resentment have flourished even three and four generations out.

This analogy may prompt the question, "Does not this writing open up the wounds afresh also?" Well—yes, it does. But if I might take a moment to draw the analogy out further, then I can make a distinction. While on my honeymoon, I dashed my finger on a rock in the ocean. It just happened to be my right ring finger and so I was obsessed with its appearance. I did not want to put a band aid on it because that would draw attention away from my beautiful rings. So I just washed it off with soap and hot water and hoped it would heal. However, after a week the wound got infected, filled with white puss, and was sore. Also, skin had started to grow over it, but had turned hard and dead because of the infection. I had to actually cut the wound back open intentionally to remove the infected part *and* to apply a healing balm to the wound. The wound healed quickly after that. It would have been quite a different and painful thing if I had scraped the same sore spot on another stone. Ultimately the spiritual answer to racism is found in God. It is He, and not "father time," who is Jehovah Rapha our healer. We need the dead skin of silence and denial to be peeled back and this heavy wound honestly re-

opened and exposed to His healing touch. He is that balm in
Gilead referred to by the prophet Jeremiah.

> For they have healed the hurt of the daughter of my people
> slightly, saying, Peace, peace; when there is no peace. . . . For
> the hurt of the daughter of my people am I hurt; I am black;
> astonishment hath taken hold on me. Is there no balm in
> Gilead; is there no physician there? Why then is not the health
> of the daughter of my people recovered? (Jeremiah 8:11,
> 21–22)

The direct connection between slavery and racism is clear
when we review the timeline of events together as an overview.
Using the graphic timeline on the following pages, let us begin at
the beginning. Most people have been led to believe that racism
always was and always will be with us. There is nothing we can
do about it because it's just a natural part of humanity. Contrary
to that popular belief, there was a *time before racism*. From the
beginning of time until approximately the 1390's A.D., there was
generally no enmity between Africans and Europeans. It was not
because there had been no contact, no interaction. In fact there
were actually European slaves in Africa as well as African slaves
in Europe before the Mid-Atlantic slave trade began. It was a
"benign" (non-racial) slavery where the dignity of the human
being was not maligned to promulgate enslavement.

> But, beloved, be not ignorant of this one thing, that one day is
> with the Lord as a thousand years, and a thousand years as one
> day. (II Peter 3:8)

How long of a time was the time before racism? Some students of the Bible would say that one could count the generations
from Jesus Christ back to Adam and thereby establish how many
years the earth has been in existence. I, however, do not ascribe
to that theory because it is not clear whether every generation is
specifically named. There may be gaps. Therefore, the time before 1440 A.D. is simply estimated at thousands and thousands
of years. One thing is clear, however, it was a long time. It was
far longer than the 400 plus years ascribed to the African holo-

caust. The good news is that our Creator is eternal. The 400 years of slavery plus the approximately 100 years since emancipation are only a glitch in history to Him. And because a thousand years to Him is like one day, we could argue that from an eternal perspective this madness has only been going on for one half of a day. That is not to say that the matter is trivial to Him. He has compassion for the oppressed. Therefore, each day of slavery was a thousand years of agony for Him. Satan's lie is that racism had no beginning and therefore has no end. It always was and always will be; therefore, we should resign ourselves to the fact that nothing can be done. Fortunately for those among us who build our hopes on things eternal, we know that this too shall pass.

Again, some who deny the problem of racism may say we should not count the last 100 years after slavery was abolished. However, there is a direct line between enslavement and defamation of culture, to peonage and sharecropping, to segregation and discrimination, to today's racial tensions revealed in redlining, hate crimes, police brutality, and an unbalanced penal justice system.

We can connect the past to the present as can be seen in the graphically illustrated timeline. The first thing to note is that the time when Jesus walked the earth falls within the *time before racism*. Therefore, what skin tone He had would *not* have been noteworthy. It is only a topic of debate today because of the Atlantic Slave Trade and the resultant racism. Next we see that the 423-year block of time where Africans were enslaved has many other blocks inside. That is because the slave trade escalated and declined gradually with many different nuances and overlapping periods within it. American slavery lasted 244 years from the time the first slave ship arrived in Jamestown in 1619 until the Emancipation Proclamation in 1863.

Legalized enslavement of "negroes" in America did not happen all of a sudden, but gradually trickled into existence. Initially black and white slaves worked side by side. Then legal protection was taken away from blacks, bit by bit. Southerners stopped allowing blacks freedom upon baptism into Christianity. The custom of keeping dark-skinned people in bondage gelled before

1440 A.D.

CENTURIES AND CENTURIES

TIME BEFORE RACISM (EURO/AFRICAN)

THOUSANDS AND THOUSANDS OF YEARS

33 A.D.
Jesus Christ is crucified and resurrected.

(Genisis 1:1)
THE BEGINNING

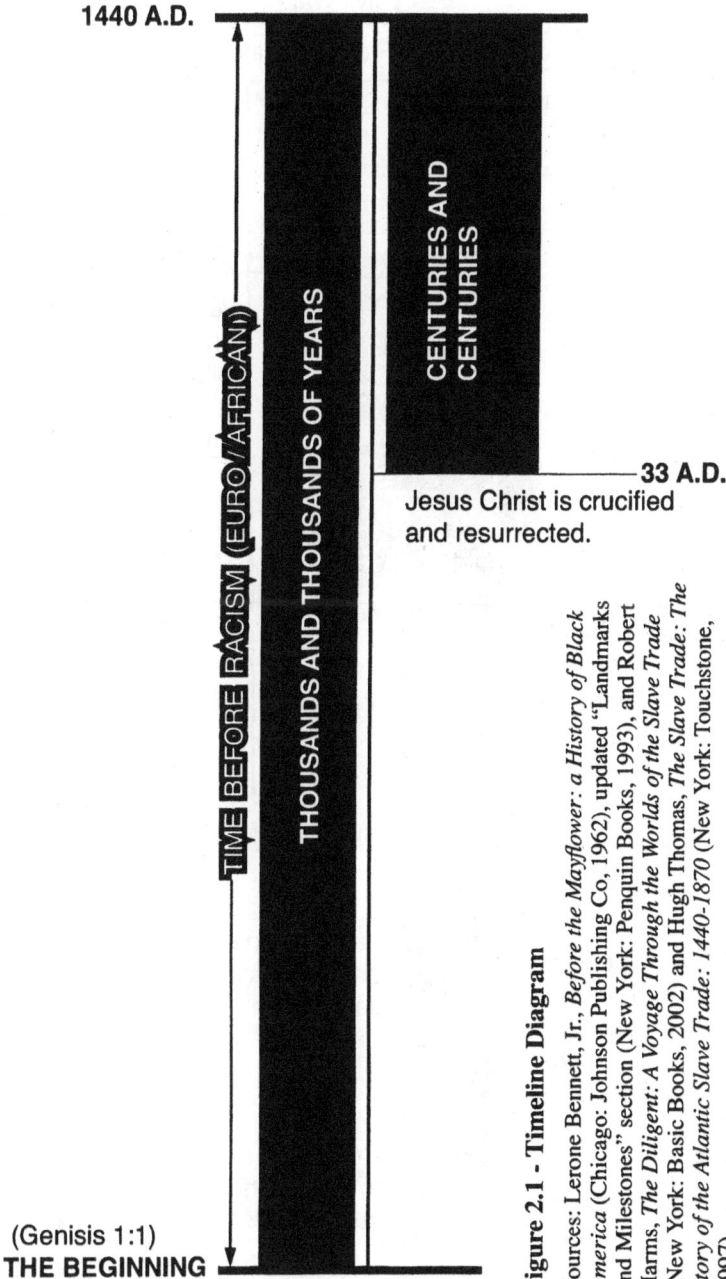

Figure 2.1 - Timeline Diagram

Sources: Lerone Bennett, Jr., *Before the Mayflower: a History of Black America* (Chicago: Johnson Publishing Co, 1962), updated "Landmarks and Milestones" section (New York: Penquin Books, 1993), and Robert Harms, *The Diligent: A Voyage Through the Worlds of the Slave Trade* (New York: Basic Books, 2002) and Hugh Thomas, *The Slave Trade: The Story of the Atlantic Slave Trade: 1440-1870* (New York: Touchstone, 1997)

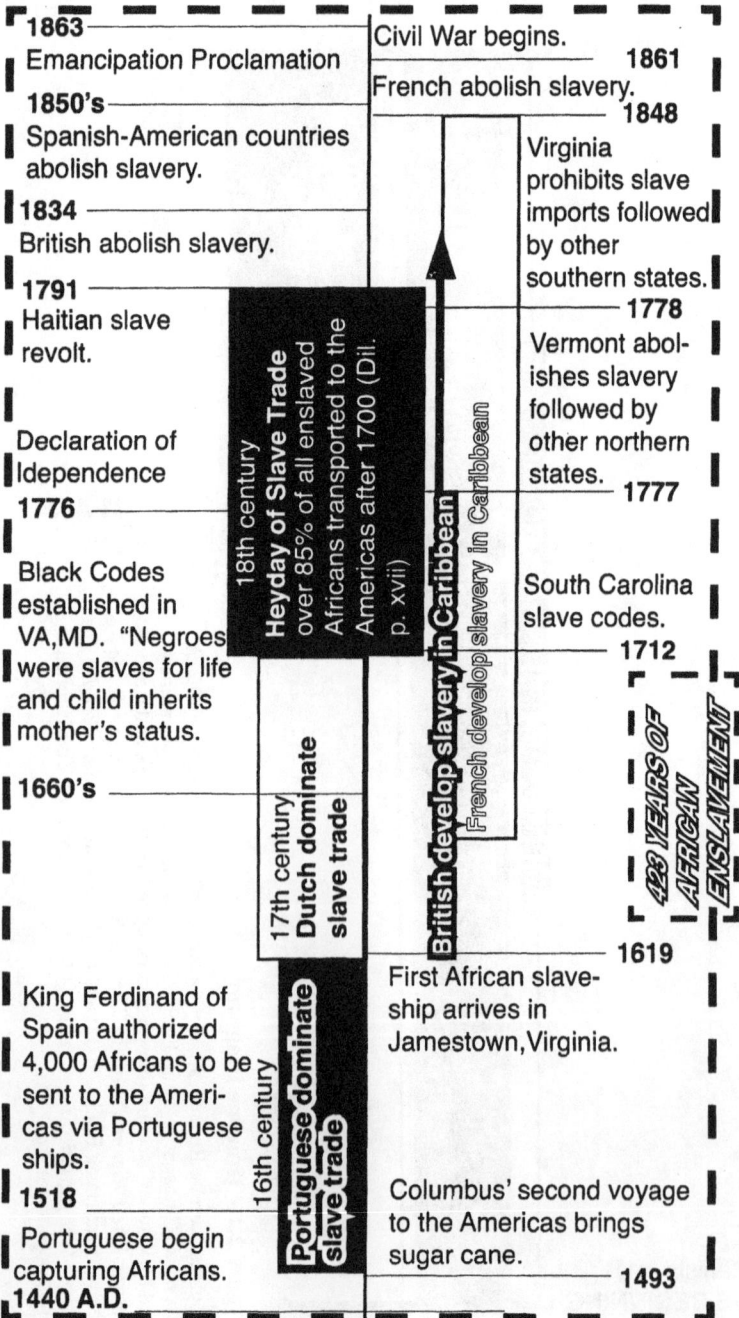

fig. 2.1-2 Time Does Not Heal All Wounds

1863 — Emancipation Proclamation

Civil War begins. **1861**

French abolish slavery. **1848**

1850's — Spanish-American countries abolish slavery.

Virginia prohibits slave imports followed by other southern states. **1778**

1834 — British abolish slavery.

1791 — Haitian slave revolt.

Vermont abolishes slavery followed by other northern states. **1777**

Declaration of Idependence **1776**

18th century Heyday of Slave Trade over 85% of all enslaved Africans transported to the Americas after 1700 (Dil. p. xvii)

British develop slavery in Caribbean

French develop slavery in Caribbean

Black Codes established in VA,MD. "Negroes were slaves for life and child inherits mother's status.

South Carolina slave codes. **1712**

1660's

17th century Dutch dominate slave trade

429 YEARS OF AFRICAN ENSLAVEMENT

1619

King Ferdinand of Spain authorized 4,000 Africans to be sent to the Americas via Portuguese ships. **1518**

First African slaveship arrives in Jamestown, Virginia.

16th century Portuguese dominate slave trade

Portuguese begin capturing Africans. **1440 A.D.**

Columbus' second voyage to the Americas brings sugar cane. **1493**

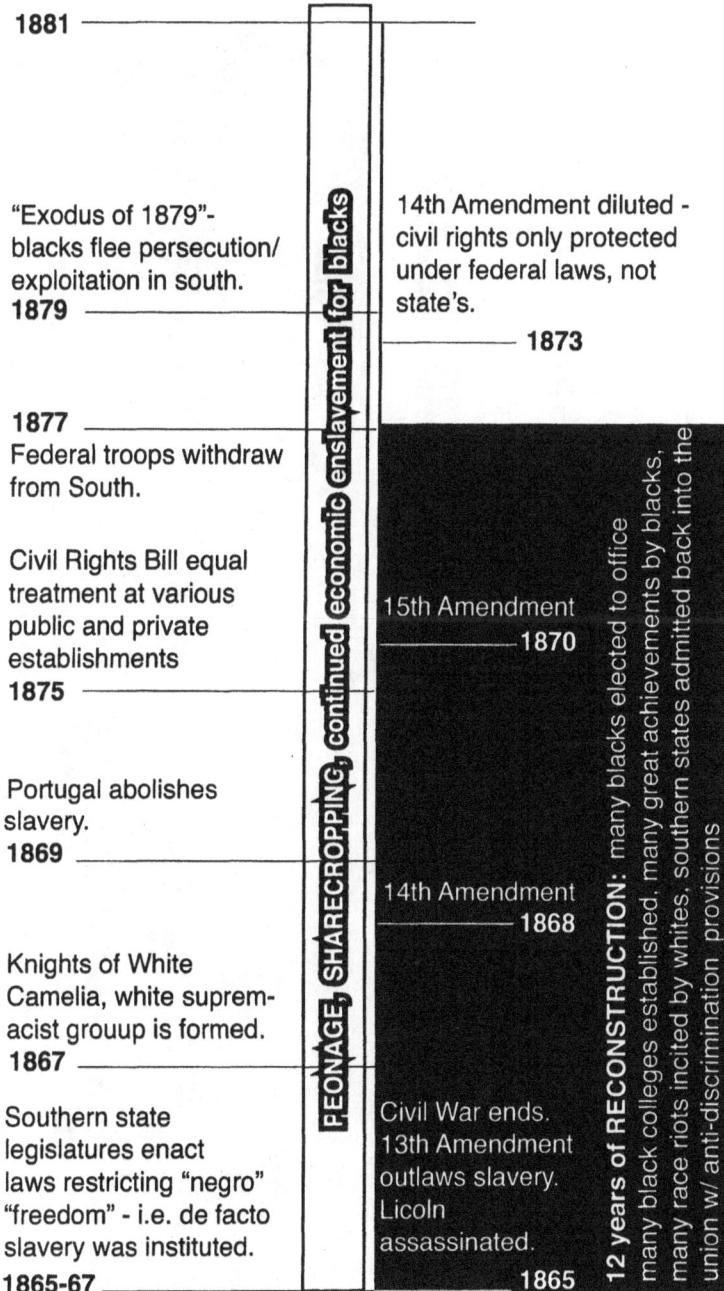

1881

"Exodus of 1879"-
blacks flee persecution/
exploitation in south.
1879

14th Amendment diluted -
civil rights only protected
under federal laws, not
state's.
————— **1873**

1877
Federal troops withdraw
from South.

Civil Rights Bill equal
treatment at various
public and private
establishments
1875

Portugal abolishes
slavery.
1869

Knights of White
Camelia, white suprem-
acist grouup is formed.
1867

Southern state
legislatures enact
laws restricting "negro"
"freedom" - i.e. de facto
slavery was instituted.
1865-67

PEONAGE, SHARECROPPING, continued economic enslavement for blacks

15th Amendment
————1870

14th Amendment
————1868

Civil War ends.
13th Amendment
outlaws slavery.
Licoln
assassinated.
1865

12 years of RECONSTRUCTION: many blacks elected to office many black colleges established. many great achievements by blacks, many race riots incited by whites. southern states admitted back into the union w/ anti-discrimination provisions

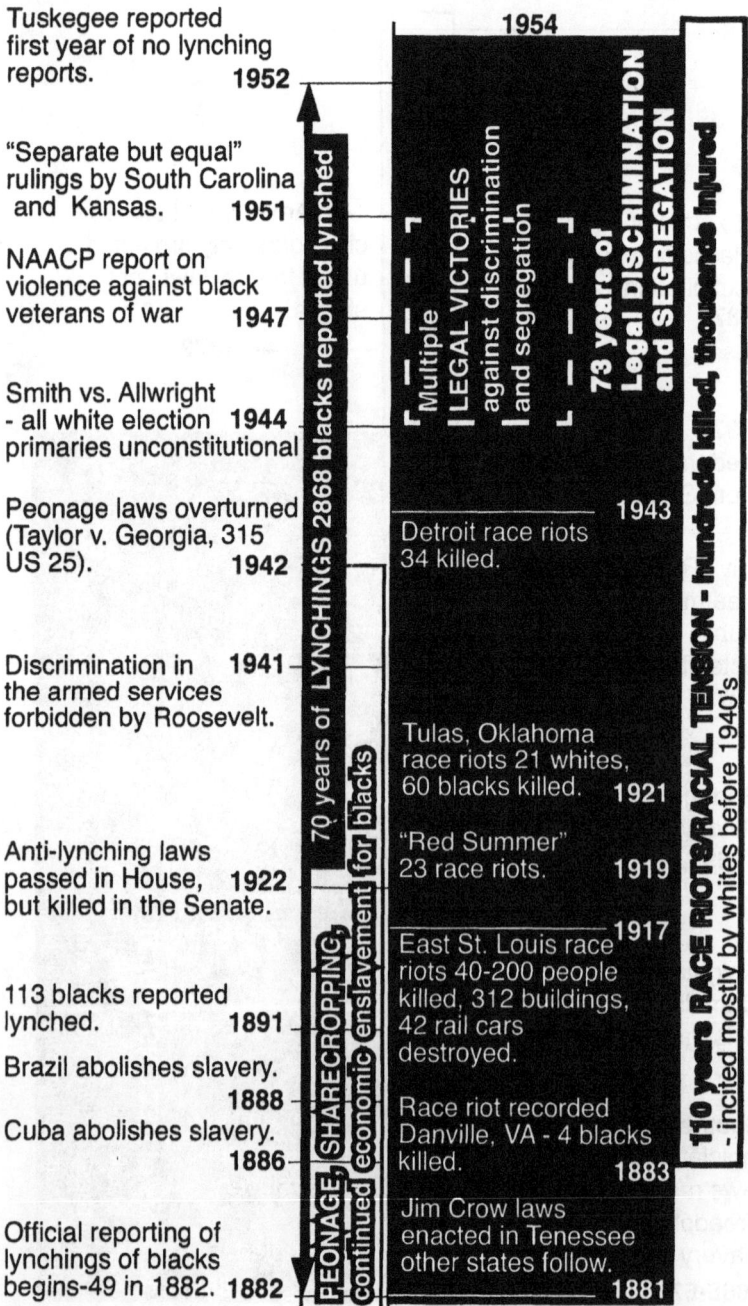

fig. 2.1-4   Time Does Not Heal All Wounds

1954

Tuskegee reported
first year of no lynching
reports.   **1952**

"Separate but equal"
rulings by South Carolina
and Kansas.   **1951**

NAACP report on
violence against black
veterans of war   **1947**

Smith vs. Allwright
- all white election **1944**
primaries unconstitutional

Peonage laws overturned
(Taylor v. Georgia, 315
US 25).   **1942**

Discrimination in   **1941**
the armed services
forbidden by Roosevelt.

Anti-lynching laws
passed in House,   **1922**
but killed in the Senate.

113 blacks reported
lynched.   **1891**

Brazil abolishes slavery.
                    1888
Cuba abolishes slavery.
                    1886

Official reporting of
lynchings of blacks
begins-49 in 1882. **1882**

70 years of LYNCHINGS 2868 blacks reported lynched

Multiple LEGAL VICTORIES against discrimination and segregation

73 years of Legal DISCRIMINATION and SEGREGATION

Detroit race riots
34 killed.   **1943**

Tulas, Oklahoma
race riots 21 whites,
60 blacks killed.   **1921**

"Red Summer"
23 race riots.   **1919**

1917
East St. Louis race
riots 40-200 people
killed, 312 buildings,
42 rail cars
destroyed.

Race riot recorded
Danville, VA - 4 blacks
killed.   **1883**

Jim Crow laws
enacted in Tenessee
other states follow.
                    1881

PEONAGE, SHARECROPPING, continued economic enslavement for blacks

110 years RACE RIOTS/RACIAL TENSION - hundreds killed, thousands injured - incited mostly by whites before 1940's

1968
Fair Housing Act,
Civil Rights Act prohibit dis-
crimination in mortgage loans.

1964
MLK wins Nobel Peace Prize.

1963 March on Washington
("I Have A Dream").
Kennedy assassinated.
Johnson signs Civil Rights
Bill into law.

1961
Freedom riders bus trip.
MLK arrested in Albany, GA
for protest marches.

1960 Civil Rights Act
MLK arrested at Atlanta
sit-in.

1958 Oklahoma City lunch
counter sit-ins.

1957 Civil Rights Act
Central High School,
Little Rock, Arkansas
is integrated.

1956 Federal ruling against
segregation on city buses
backed by Supreme Court

1955
Rosa Parks sparks
Montgomery Bus Boycott.

1955 14 year old
Emmitt Tilll kidnapped,
mauled, lynched.

1954 Brown v. Board
of Education - segregation in
public schools unconstitutional

CIVIL RIGHTS ERA, 10 more years of legal battles

1968
MLK assassinated,
riots in 140 cities.

1967
75 race riots,
83 people killed.

1966
23 race riots,
11 people killed.

1965 West Side of
Chicago riots
National Gaurd called in

1964
7 major race riots.

Trumbull Park Housing
riots - police state to
keep order.
1953-56

110 years RACE RIOTS/RACIAL TENSION - hundreds killed, thousands injured - incited mostly by whites before 1940's

fig. 2.1-6   Time Does Not Heal All Wounds

1980's, 90's, today
Various police brutality cases, police and prosecutorial misconduct Related protests.

1997 Geronimo Pratt - biased murder conviction overturned after 27 years in prison. Many similar cases in1970's, 80's, 90's, 00's

1997 Abner Luima brutalized by NYPD

1991 Rodney King beating by 4 white policemen is televised

1989- Redlining controversy - sparked by HMDA ammenment to require reporting of race of mortgage loan applicants

1989
Yusef Hawkins killed by white mob in Bensonhurst, NY

1986 Michael Griffeth killed by white mob in Howard Beach, NY

1983 Record high unemployment for blacks = 20.8%

1975 Home Mortgage Disclosure Act (HMDA)

1971
Highest unemployment for blacks since depression.

1971
Supreme Court ruling to integrate schools through busing.

TAINTED JUSTICE - overturned convictions, police brutality, racial profiling . . .

REDLINING, ECONOMIC DISPARITY between blacks/whites (continues)

1995 O.J. Simpson found not guilty of murdering white wife
Racial tension, controveries ensue.

1992
Simi Valley verdict aquits white officers in Rodney King beating.
Major riots nationwide.

1980 Ronald Reagan elected president.
Race Riots - Idabell, OK 2 people killed.
Major race riot - Miami 16 people killed, 300 injured.
State troopers called to racial disturbances in cities in 5 states.

1979 Sharp rise in KKK activity Klansman kills 5 in anti-Klan rally - Greensboro, NC.

1977 Roots - television series about slavery 130 million viewers.

1974 Boston school busing crisis National Guard

1971 Race riots Wilmington, NC National Guard - 2 killed
Race riots Chattanooga, TN National Guard - 1 killed 400 arrested

RACE RIOTS/RACIAL TENSION - hundreds killed, thousands injured - 110 years & counting . .

it was written into law. In the 1660's Maryland and Virginia wrote the first statutes that made "negroes" slaves for life and made the child to inherit the mother's condition. In other words, perpetual slavery for blacks was established. This sin became a corporate sin upon this nation when slavery was given the official stamp of approval by being passed into the laws of the land. The 3/5th compromise in the Constitution said that a slave counted as 3/5th of a person for purposes of census and taxation of slave owners. With that legislation America greatly damaged the psyche of every black person in the nation and the perception of us as not full human beings ripples on today. In fact the pseudo-science movement is still bent on proving that erroneous categorization. Even after the 14th Amendment to the Constitution was passed, which outlawed denying "any person of life, liberty, or property, without due process of law," southern states persisted in instituting and legislating segregation and discrimination.

After emancipation, the Reconstruction era began. Blacks achieved many great things during this era, however, that only lasted for 12 years, which ended when the federal troops withdrew from the South and persecution of black people resumed and escalated. During that time there was also rioting, incited by whites, and the economic oppression of "freed" blacks began with the enactment of peonage laws and sharecropping.

Although they were not called slavery, the post-Reconstruction Southern practices of peonage, forced convict labor, and to a lesser degree sharecropping essentially continued the institution of slavery well into the twentieth century, and were in some ways even worse. (Peonage, for example, was a complex system in which a black man would be arrested for "vagrancy," another word for unemployment, ordered to pay a fine he could not afford, and incarcerated. A plantation owner would pay his fine and "hire" him until he could afford to pay off the fine himself: The peon was then forced to work, locked up at night, and, if he ran away, chased by bloodhounds until recaptured. One important difference between peonage and slavery was that while slaves had considerable monetary value for the plantation owner, peons had almost none, and could therefore be mistreated—and even murdered —without monetary loss.) —Yuval Taylor [5]

The devaluing of black life Taylor described is corroborated by the official reports of the lynching of black men that began to crop up less than two decades after slavery was abolished. Around the same time, Jim Crow laws were established to make it officially known that this nation still considered black people less than human.

Some date the beginning of the Jim Crow era even earlier than the timeline presented here indicates because, just like slavery, it was unwritten law even before it was written on the books. Beginning in the early 1870's Southerners attempted to degrade and dehumanize black life through minstrel shows depicting blacks as inferior. The term "Jim Crow" originate from a song performed by a white minstrel entertainer named Daddy Rice who would cover his face with charcoal and make stereotypical racists jests about blacks. But it wasn't simply a poking of fun because white southerners imposed segregation by threat both before and after it was written into law. Officially this era began after the Compromise of 1877 when the president of the United States, Rutherford Hayes, promised to end the Reconstruction era. The federal government pulled out of the south and ceased to actively protect the rights of black people as stated in the 14th Amendment. These laws stated explicitly that blacks, although technically citizens, were considered second-class citizens. They could be barred from and/or separated in public spaces. The most far-reaching aspect was that these laws denied black men the right to vote. This era was a time of terrorism against the black community through lynching and white-incited rioting to protect the color line. The Jim Crow era coincides with the unfair practices of peonage and sharecropping. These atrocities lasted until the early 1950's, *which is only 50 years prior to the time of this writing.*

Looking again at the diagram we see that overlapping this period and continuing today are 109 years and counting of race riots in America. That term, "race riots," has connotations today of angry, out of control, black people protesting some racial injustice. However, it is noteworthy that most of these riots were incited by white people before the 1940's, and that it was mostly blacks who were harmed or threatened by them.[6] Just like the angry white lynch mobs who forced many a black man out of his home into the woods to be terrorized, mauled, and then hanged from a tree, the riotous mob's goal was to intimidate blacks in order keep them from enjoying the benefits of full American citizenship.

Next we see the Civil Rights victory won when segregation in public schools was ruled illegal (Brown v. Board of Education). This can be seen as the end of legal segregation. However, the enactment of the law and the enforcement of it were two different hurdles. Thus we have almost a whole decade of continued Civil Rights battles and turmoil, from 1954 to 1963, which was geared toward ending segregation and discrimination.

Connecting that dot to the place where we are today in the struggle against racism is the most difficult line to convince people of. Many who do not believe we still have a struggle on our hands would say the picture was completed. Everything came full circle and was resolved during the Civil Rights battles of the 50's and 60's. However school desegregation, or busing, continued well into the 1970's. It was one of the main prompts behind the "white flight" to the suburbs that was mentioned earlier. With the next decade came an era of backlash to Civil Rights that was ushered in when president Ronald Reagan took office in 1980. While it is true that there were no more *legal* obstacles to racial equality after the Civil Rights era, the disparity between whites and blacks in this country still exists. The lives of black people today have been influenced by the legacy of slavery. The same holds true for white people, though not in the same way.

I grew up in the northern state of Connecticut and remember vividly the trips our family made to visit relatives in the south. As a child, I never knew why we traveled with so much food. Or why when we got to certain areas, we would not stop to use public restrooms, but instead would pull to the side of the road, open the car doors and drape them with blankets while we relieved ourselves. Later in life, I realized that it was because the bitterness of Jim Crow lingered. Although we could *legally* use facilities in those areas, or eat in their restaurants, it really was not worth the hassle or worth risking our safety and our lives. At least my parents did not think so. They were both born in the late 1930's and grew up during a time of racial turmoil over Civil Rights as well as the continuation of lynching and race riots. To say that I, representing the next generation of blacks, was not influenced by their outlook, their fears, and their doubts is preposterous. Also, I recall when busing began in order to integrate the public school system. I remember vividly the first time I was called a derogatory name by my fellow white classmates.

When I was in second grade my well-intentioned teacher went around the classroom and asked everyone to share something about their ethnic heritage, their family background. Panic and fear overtook me because I had no clue what to say. There was an Indian boy in the class and he went before me. Since his skin tone seemed the closest to mine, I just said I was Indian. The teacher questioned my answer and then said that we should all go home and ask our grandparents or older relatives about our family history. When I went to my grandmother and asked her, she adamantly refused to talk about her past. I pleaded with her and told her it was for a school assignment. But she insisted that I did not want to know all of that stuff and it was better that I should never know. That incident influenced me as a small child to believe that my heritage and ancestors were a dark mystery, something to be ashamed of and hidden away. It was not until I got to graduate school and my studies broadened to include all of the cultures of the world that I began to think differently.

Racism has not ended by any stretch of the imagination. I would argue, in fact, that the most daunting battle of all is still ahead and close at hand. The social and economic struggles do continue still. And we do have disparity in the justice and penal system because of the legacy of slavery. However, the biggest battle looming on the horizon is spiritual. The line connecting the Civil Rights era to this current struggle is something that has been intangibly passed from one generation to the next. Now is the time for spiritual warfare and in this realm, and the enemy is as subtle as a snake.

Before going into the details of things spiritual, however, there is one more argument that needs to be considered. Even after being convinced that there is a connection between slavery and racism, some would still downplay this issue saying that many peoples around the world have also suffered discrimination. What about the Jews in Nazi Germany? Or the Kurdish peoples in Iraq? Or the Irish, or the Italians when they first came to America? Why do others seem to have overcome while blacks continue to hang on to the pain?

One reason, which we have already brought to light, is the longevity of slavery and discrimination in America. It affected many, many generations in such a way as to destroy African culture wholesale. That differentiates it from other racial atrocities that lasted no more than one generation.[7] Add to the longevity the severity and the gravity of slavery in America and you see the clear distinction between the African holocaust and other ethnic atrocities. Let us review details of a life of slavery. Please know that the intention here is not to elicit pity, nor is it intended to encourage black people to wallow in self-pity or tout our suffering as a badge of honor. These details are just reminders of the low depth to which America fell in order to understand the magnitude of spiritual battle needed to overcome this situation.

Overall slaves in America suffered loss of personal freedom, personal goals and dreams. It is a well-documented, well-recognized fact that families were split up for reasons of profit. Mothers had children torn from them. Husbands, wives and close family members were separated and sold away. Because of these and other wrongs, there was psychological and social damage done to enslaved African peoples in America. I cannot fully cover the socio-psychological aspect here because it is too extensive. Others have done exhaustive writing on this subject.[8] The role of the man and woman and the relationship of children to parents were destroyed and distorted. The man had no means to provide for his family, no control over his own efforts, no authority and no contribution in society. He therefore could not command respect from his wife or children. The woman, being treated like a child herself, likewise could not command respect from children. Family values, the effects of family incidences, and family history are passed down spiritually from generation to generation.

Fear was the overriding emotion that slaves had toward whites. Not even anger or resentment topped this.[9] I can hardly imagine life under this type of mental anguish. One personal analogy I can draw, however, is to the sniper incident that my family and I lived through. In the fall of 2002 our state, Maryland, along with the state of Virginia, and DC were under attack by a sniper who was shooting people at random almost every day. He managed to evade capture for almost a month. During that time the level of anxiety and fear in the community was intense. People were afraid to go and get gas or to venture out of the house for any reason. People were running to their cars and walking zigzag when they were out in the open. This is but a fraction of the anxiety that slaves and also blacks living under the shadow of lynching and peonage endured—*for hundreds of years*.

The typical workday for a slave lasted from sunrise to sunset, six days a week. There were very few exceptions. A ten to fifteen minute break for lunch was standard. Sometimes when the moon was bright enough, slaves were forced to work at night. When they got "home" from the fields, there were still their own personal chores to do.[10] On sugar plantations conditions were even worse. The workday typically lasted 16–18 hours, seven days a week![11]

The food allotment for a slave was "a peck of cornmeal and 3–4 lbs. of salt pork or bacon" per adult per week. Only on special occasions like Christmas and weddings were they allowed other foods. Imagine the drudgery of eating the same thing every meal, everyday—*all of your life*. Knowing what we know now about nutrition makes this even more egregious. One writer described it as "sufficient bulk, but improper balance."[12]

On a Maryland farm where Frederick Douglas was a child, "the corn-meal mush . . . was placed in a large wooden tray. . . . This tray was set down, either on the floor of the kitchen, or out or doors on the ground; and the children were called, . . . and like so many pigs would come, and literally devour the mush—some with oyster shells, some with pieces of shingles, and none with spoons." In Africa the Negro had rarely consumed his food with less dignity and grace than this.[13]

Also, in the writings of Fanny Kemble, the wife of a Georgia plantation owner, she noted that "slaves approached her almost daily to beg for rice or meat."[14] The psychological damage done to a person who has to beg for a morsel of meat from someone for whom he has work 12–18 hours a day without pay is unarguably tremendous.

Clothing was even more of a degradation and was a health issue as well. It was more costly than food, which led to slave's clothing being worn out and shabby. In winter this posed a health threat and in warmer months it was simply shameful and a disgrace.[15]

As a child in Maryland, Frederick Douglass "was kept almost in a state of nudity; no shoes, no stockings, no jacket, no trousers; nothing but coarse sack-cloth or tow-linen, made into a sort of shirt, reaching down to my knees. This I wore night and day, changing it once a week."[16]

The provision for shelter was even worse because, as it was the most costly part of keeping slaves. It was generally cramped, dirty, cold, and dark. Windows were rare because of the cost of glass. However there were many openings as the construction tended to be shoddy. Even those openings would be blocked, as best the slaves could block them, for insulation purposes.[17]

With regard to mortality rates, the 1850 census reported the average life span for "negroes" to be 21.4 years. For whites it was 25.5 years. However, many slave's deaths went unreported and these statistics did not include infant deaths.[18] From some of the scant surviving records on infant mortality we see a very high death rate. One plantation's records showed 16 infant deaths out of 24 live births. That is a 67% death rate. Another showed 29 out of 55 babies born had died giving a 53% rate.[19] "These statistics," notes Kenneth Stampp, "discredit one of the traditions about slavery days: that a substantial number of aged 'aunties' and 'uncles' spent their declining years as pensioners living leisurely and comfortably on their masters' bounty."[20]

These are some of the details of a slave's life that leave vivid impressions and help us understand this atrocity on a personal level. In America, black people endured this for 244 years. It was harsh on the body, spirit and mind. It does have heavy implications for us today. When slavery ended America's reaction to it varied and changed over time. The southern states of this nation initially were in disbelief that this era of exploitation was actually over. While they pondered the revised status of former slaves, the rest of the nation pondered what to do about the "negro problem" in America. Then came the era of segregation and discrimination against blacks throughout the country as well as the terrorism in the south. Next came the era of legal and political struggle. Now, only 40 years out from the Civil Rights era, this nation is mainly in denial that there is any problem remaining. Mainstream America would be content if slavery was never mentioned again. There is a prevailing sweep-it-under-the-rug mentality.

But alas silence like a cancer grows. Un-repented sin festers and manifests itself in unusual and harmful ways. It turns into iniquity. Iniquity is a sin that goes unchecked for so long that it becomes a part of you. You assume it is natural and normal even. It seems to have no end and you do not recognize its beginning. This is how the sin of slavery has evolved (for lack of a better term) into the iniquity of racism today. There is a false and very delicate peace maintained in our society through pluralism and politeness. Some of us simply tolerate one another with a distant politeness while anger and resentment seethe just below the surface. We can point to images of racial harmony that we see on TV, to the integrated workplace, and to intermarriage between blacks and whites as indications that we have overcome this sin. While individuals may have overcome racial obstacles in their personal relationships, and while this is a wonderful and commendable thing, as a body of people however, we remain stained. To deny that there is a problem is to turn a blind eye, to maintain an ignorant ear, and to apply a lying tongue to the situation.

On the other hand, there are great rewards to be had by tackling this issue bravely and honestly. The number one and most important reward is that it would be pleasing to God. If the truth shames the devil, as the saying goes, then it obviously exalts God. I believe it would also have earthly benefits. If there were no racism would there not also be less crime in our cities? If black people did not feel relegated to second-class citizenship, would it not soothe much anger, aggression, and rebellion in predominantly black communities? Less crime, even the perception of less crime, would lead to less fear. Less fear would lead to less waste of our lands and resources as mentioned earlier. This would also please God because although this earth is His and the fullness thereof, He has entrusted us, mankind, with stewardship over the land. Imagine what the eradication of racism would mean for your neighborhood, your city, your state, this nation, and even the world!

Visualize our nation with just and equitable systems. Instead of inner-city schools being broken down facilities using antiquated tools, they could be vibrant places of learning on par with suburban schools. They would produce well-educated students eager to participate in and contribute to a stable economy. If the justice system were racially just and the penal system was not disproportionately filled with black men and women, then there would not be such a shadow of doubt cast over every conviction and every death sentence issued. Think of the workplace. Racial tensions would not cloud the air over every national issue. Relationships and friendships could continue on unthreatened.

Finally, brethren, whatsoever things are true, whatsoever things are honest, whatsoever things are just, whatsoever things are pure, whatsoever things are lovely, whatsoever things are of good report; if there be any virtue, and if there be any praise, think on these things. (Philippians 4:8)

Chapter Two Endnotes

1. Hugh Thomas, *The Slave Trade: The Story of the Atlantic Slave Trade: 1440–1870* (New York, NY: Touchstone, 1997), 11.
2. Published by U.S. Department of Justice, Office of Justice Program, Bureau of Justice Statistics, "Personal Crimes of Violence, 2000," Table 27.
3. Howard N. Snyder, PH.D, "Sexual Assault of Young Children as Reported to Law Enforcement: Victim, Incident, and Offender Characteristics," *NCJ182990* (National Center for Juvenile Justice, July, 2000) 2.
4. Unchecked by man. God has authority over even Satan's activities.
5. Yuval Taylor, ed. *I was Born A Slave (vol. 1)*. (Chicago: Lawrence Hill, 1999), quoted in Randall Robinson, *The Debt: What America Owes to Blacks*, (New York: Penguin Putnam, Inc., 2000) 226.
6. Lerone Bennett, *Before the Mayflower: a History of Black America*, (Chicago: Johnson Publishing Co., 1962), updated "Landmarks and Milestones" section (New York: Penquin Books, 1993), 486–550.
7. Randall Robinson, *The Debt: What America Owes to Blacks* (New York: Penguin Putnam, Inc., 2000) 52 & Chapter 1.
8. Many black people today are like myself and have studied these books avidly. In fact it is a consuming passion for many of us. I would guess that the majority of white people have not read about or even given much thought to this subject, nor studied avidly these types of books. Therefore, whenever this issue comes up for discussion multicultural settings there is again complete conflict between the black and white perspectives.
9. Kenneth Stampp, *The Peculiar Institution: Slavery in the Ante-Bellum South* (New York: Alfred A. Knofp, Inc., 1956) 146 & 381.
10. Stampp, *The Peculiar Institution*, 74.
11. Stampp, *The Peculiar Institution*, 85.
12. Stampp, *The Peculiar Institution*, 282.
13. Stampp, *The Peculiar Institution*, 288–289.
14. Stampp, *The Peculiar Institution*, 286.
15. Stampp, *The Peculiar Institution*, 289–292.
16. Stampp, *The Peculiar Institution*, 291.
17. Stampp, *The Peculiar Institution*, 292–295.
18. Stampp, *The Peculiar Institution*, 318.

19. Stampp, *The Peculiar Institution*, 320.
20. Stampp, *The Peculiar Institution*, 318.

Chapter Three

Pride—The Root Cause

Now that we have explored *how* we got where we are today and hopefully are convinced that the plant has sprung from the seed, we ask the question *why*. Why did all of this happen? The roots of racism are slavery, but what is the root of slavery? An honest assessment of this question will shed light on the solution. Knowing as much as possible about the enemy is important in any battle. Eradicating racism is a battle. Therefore, let us now examine how it germinated and what foe concocted this scheme. At the start of my research and writing, I had preconceived notions about the root cause. After a great deal of prayer and research, I found none of my preconceptions to be fully correct and some were just completely false. They were all too simple to explain such a complex dilemma as racism. I found that the root cause was greed fueled by the mother of all sin—PRIDE. It is simply said, but actually complex. There was the prideful greed of the African kidnappers who delivered their neighbors into bondage for pay. Then there was greedy pride of the European slave financiers, merchants, and slavers who disregarded all human dignity in the name of profit. The competition to produce and the superiority complex developed in the Americas is unparalleled in modern times and was also the result of foolish pride.

Initially I thought greed alone was the spiritual sickness at the root. However, after more prayerful study, I found that it was coupled with and even driven by pride—a thing that God hates. (Proverbs 6:16)

"According to Christian teachers, the essential vice, the utmost evil, is Pride."[1] Pride makes a person want more than his neighbor has—regardless of how much that is. Here is how Christian apologist C.S. Lewis explained it:

> Pride is essentially competitive—is competitive by its very nature—while the other vices are competitive only, so to speak, by accident. Pride gets no pleasure out of having something, only out of having more of it than the next man.[2]
>
> What is it that makes a political leader or a whole nation go on and on, demanding more and more? Pride again. Pride is competitive by its very nature: that is why it goes on and on.[3]

So while a greedy African might look at the profit he could gain by kidnapping his neighbor and selling him, if he saw another kidnapping hundreds and building an empire, there is where he would set his goal. If the people in one city in France saw the prosperity of another because it was a slave port, then their mission in building a slave port would be to rival the first. They would want to have just as much pride in their town, after all, as the next. The American slave owner could drive his slaves to work all day long, but if his neighbor decided to make his work by moonlight the first American would be tempted to follow suit. He would not want his neighbor to gain advantage over him. He would not want to feel inferior to his neighbor, or worry that his neighbor was getting ahead of him in the game of getting. Then there is the general pride of racism, which is apart from greed, that whispers in the white man's ear, "You are better than the black man—by nature."

There are some common misconceptions about what caused racism to begin. Before going in depth into pride, the sin that started it all, let us examine some of those erroneous thoughts.

Misconception #1:

The invention of the gun was the root cause of slavery. I initially thought that if I could just identify that original evil-minded inventor of this killing machine along with his cohorts then I could identify where humanity went wrong and became racist. My theory was that this man or group of men invented the gun and immediately saw that it would give Europeans advantage over Africans. Then they conjured a diabolical plot to terrorize and exploit the innocent African people. They grew in their following inspiring many other Europeans to do the same, thus the birth of racism.

Upon further investigation I found that this myth is only partly true. It is true that guns did facilitate wars that created dissension which in turn led to increased slave trading. For example, the Owu War, which lasted from about 1818 to 1825 can be attributed to the high demand for slaves. The Owu were being kidnapped and sold to Europeans by the Ife and Ijebu people. Therefore, they lodged counterattacks. This war is noteworthy because it is the first extensive use of firearms in combat in Africa.[4]

Guns were also a major factor in the transformation of Africa's Gold Coast into the Slave Coast, when they turned from exporting mostly gold to exporting mostly human beings.[5] But even though the gun was a factor, it was not the root. The gun was an offshoot product of slavery that generated profit similar to sugar cane and cotton. For example, the town of Birmingham, England flourished and became famous because of gun manufacturing. In fact in 1729, the price of a slave was measured in Birmingham guns.[6] It is also noteworthy that the heyday of the slave trade was in the 1700's, the same century that gun innovation exploded.

The gun does differ from the other products of profit derived from the slave trade in that it is a weapon, a murder weapon. Therefore it has a more sinister weight and could easily be misconstrued as the root cause. However, while guns were a factor in the enslavement of Africans, the idea that armed Europeans went into Africa themselves, caught the people by surprise with this unknown weaponry and thereby kidnapped them is essentially untrue.

Misconception #2

White people naturally hated black people upon first contact. This misconception is based also on the lie that Europeans and Africans "evolved" separately until that fateful day when the first Europeans "discovered" Africa. Immediately they felt repulsion, believed themselves to be superior, and therefore set out to conquer Africa and take the people into bondage. They had guns and the zeal of evil intent propelled them to go through the continent killing, stealing, and destroying.

Again, this misconception is based on the false presupposition that Africans and Europeans never crossed paths until one day the Portuguese "discovered" Africa. There is evidence to the contrary. According to the Bible, we started out together. All of humanity sprang from Adam and Eve. We also learn from the Bible that God did not separate us into races at some point, either. Therefore, trying to find the "first" encounter is pointless. We will explore this Biblically in later chapters, but we do have extra-Biblical historical proof to corroborates this truth. For example, the Asian banana was cultivated in Africa long before it was in Europe.[7] Therefore, Africans must have traveled far and wide even before the slave trade and were not, as is commonly thought, living in the darkness of the African jungle unbeknownst to the world and vice versa. Ivan Van Sertima, a professor at Rutgers University, has researched and written extensively on how Africans even traveled to the Americas, influencing American culture even before European travelers first arrived.[8] Admittedly, at the point in time when the slave trade began, there were many Africans who were not world travelers. In fact many had not ever seen Europeans until they got onto slave ships.[9] But the same is true for some of the European slavers. However, we cannot make the broad and wrong assumption that it was always this way for all Africans in all nations. Even as late as the mid 15th century, Africans (both slave and free) integrated without incident into Spanish society.[10] Dark and light skinned peoples had intermingled without any malevolence until racism began.

Before the slave trade, dark skin was not considered an ugly or bad trait either. In the Bible King Solomon, whose reign began in 970 B.C., refers to his lover, Sheba, as black and beautiful (Song of Solomon 1:5). Herodotus, a 4th century B.C. historian from Halicarnassus (Asia Minor), who traveled the Nile River in his day is another example. He referred to the Ethiopians as "'the most handsome of peoples.'"[11]

Thus to determine the beginning of animosity between people with more melanin in their skin and those with less melanin comes not by determining when Africans and Europeans met, but rather when the seed of aversion was planted, when was it planted and also how did it grow? Referring back to the timeline illustration we are reminded again that the Mid-Atlantic slave trade had a certain beginning, and then gradually crept into the monumental historical horror that now overshadows us.

Misconception #3

The Organization to Hate Africans began racism. I imagined that this organization was founded and fueled by some sinister Hitler-like leader. If I could just find that first evildoer who succumbed to Satan's racial tempting, I could expose his life and where he went wrong. Then we could all see how to avoid such temptation and demagoguery again. But there was no one person. As already mentioned, the exact origin of the hate is fuzzy and then the sin crept. It is true that later, in the 19th century, racists did organize and used the theory of evolution and pseudoscience to try to justify the injustice of racism.

But basically, the theory of white supremacy trickled into existence in stages. First there were sporadic mentions of disdain for African people. Who knows when it started, but it culminated in the beginning of the Atlantic slave trade. These were isolated incidents that had no widespread effect. The next stage is the duration of the slave trade from its inception until emancipation.

Finally, after emancipation, there was a tremendous push to justify this great injustice through "concrete" proof that blacks are inferior to whites.

One example from the first stage of the existence of racism are writings by Fray Martín Alfonso de Córdoba, an Augustinian friar. In 1460, he authored a book called *A Garden of Noble Maidens* (a guide for young ladies) that was commissioned by the throne and read by Queen Isabella the Catholic of Spain as a young impressionable girl. In the book Córdoba writes, "'the barbarians are those who live without the law; the Latins, those who have the law; for it is the law of nations that men who live and are ruled by law shall be lords of those who have none. Wherefore they may seize and enslave them, because they are by nature the slaves of the wise.' . . . [This book] influenced [Queen Isabella's] attitude [toward] black and Moorish slaves."[12] She played a pivotal role in advancing the slave trade during her subsequent rule.

A few centuries later, around 1716, when the Atlantic slave trade was on the verge of its peak years, a French statesman named Gérard Mellier published some writings that set the tone for racist thinking of the day. In his report, *On the Commerce of Nantes and Ways to Increase It*, he said, "'the nègres are naturally inclined toward theft, larceny, lust, laziness, and treason. . . . In general, they are suited only to live in servitude and cultivate the fields of our colonies in America.'"[13] In this pivotal writing, he also promoted the lie that slavery was the path to salvation for African captives because they thereby came into contact with Christians and the gospel of Christ. This man, never having gone to the colonies or been on a slave ship to witness the horrors firsthand, clearly was only interested in boosting the economy of the seaport town of Nantes.[14] However looking back historically we see what a milestone in racist thinking he set. He also disseminated the misinformed notion that African nations were overpopulated and by that reasoning the slave trade was beneficial to them. He did not acknowledge that Africans had a variety of ways they dealt with prisoners of war besides selling them into slavery.[15] He did admit, however, that slavery was "'driven by greed and afflicted with inhumanity' and caused people to be

treated like cattle,'" but that conviction was not enough to overcome his or his audience's greedy pride.[16]

There are other examples like Mellier and Queen Isabella,
powerful people who influenced the thinking of the day. However, there is no one person or group who can be seen as the
clear leader and catalyst in this atrocity called racism. Also we
cannot heap all the blame on the souls of the leaders of the day.
Something sinister stewed in the heart of every man who sought
to gain from slavery, from the lowliest deck hand on the slave
ship, to the financiers, to the kidnappers, to the buyers.

Misconception #4:

Africans were somehow meant to be slaves. That is why the
first captives were so docile, so very naïve, and acquiesced so
easily. Why else did they not see where all this was leading and
unite against European invasion? How did the word African become synonymous with slave? Is there something about the
physical nature of black people that would make us more inclined to hard labor? Were we enslaved because we are somehow mentally and spiritually inferior? This misconception is a
very common one and one that I consciously rejected and was
reluctant to mention for reasons of personal dignity. Nevertheless these doubts kept plaguing the back of my mind, which
prompted me to explore them more in depth herein.

There is no need to look further than the Bible to see that
other peoples besides Africans have been enslaved. The Israelites were enslaved for approximately 400 years until God
brought them up out of Egypt in around 1460 B.C. Also, in the
New Testament book of Philemon, which was written around 60
A.D. we see Paul pleading for the emancipation of a slave named
Onesimus. Just a glance at secularly recorded history confirms
also that many different societies have been forced into slavery,
including the French, Germans, Spaniards, and the English.
Greeks and Romans relied heavily on slave labor to accomplish
some of their greatest achievements as well as for the routine
tasks of daily living.[17] It is notable that in 1318 A.D., Russia and

Sardinia were key sources for slaves.[18] Even closer to the dawn of the Mid-Atlantic slave trade, around the middle of the 14th century, slaves of all different skin tones were popular in Portugal and Spain.[19] Slavery, therefore, is not exclusive to Africans.

A subset of this misconception is the false idea there were no attempts to combat enslavement until the Civil War. Did black people not have the desire, or maybe the courage until that time? Were they just content being slaves? No. The truth is that the struggle was continuous from the time of capture on the shores of Africa, through the Middle Passage, and enslavement in the Americas. One witness of Africans not only defending themselves but going on the offense in this battle to steal men was recorded by the director of a popular African slave port called Whydah. He was a Frenchman named Dupetival and in 1738 he wrote, "'The Negro nations who see that we kidnap their compatriots take vengeance on the ships that send their longboats ashore and massacre all those whom they capture.'"[20] So Africans did not just go quietly into bondage. There were many incidences of African reaction to the kidnappings.

When the slave trade was on the verge of its crescendo (in the 1700's), Africans did begin also to see the dangerous foundation that was being laid in terms of dark and light skinned people of the world. William Smith, a British surveyor, wrote in 1727 that African people "'live in peace with all their neighbors and account Europeans their only enemies.'"[21] Now this is not entirely true because there were wars between African nations. However there did begin to be a tension and fear during the trading process because Africans selling others could be kidnapped themselves during the transaction. Also, Africans began to kidnap European traders in retaliation. This practice was called 'panyarring.'[22]

Add to this resistance at the shores of Africa, all of the slave ship revolts during the treacherous crossing and those uprisings that occurred in the Americas. Compound that by the widespread incidences of run-away slaves. By no means does one get the picture of complacency or acceptance of this situation by black people at any time, even though slavery had a long duration.

Overall black people never acquiesced to the situation. They always maintained hope. We still do today.

Misconception #5

God let this happen to black people as a punishment or a curse. This wrong concept is closely related to the previous one. Somehow it is the fault of the abused that they were abused. There was just something in their nature which encouraged mistreatment. Perhaps it was fate, or God's hand. This theory abdicates everyone involved of the wrong they did and is therefore very popular. People have even invented a boldfaced lie to say that black people have a "Hamitic" curse on us that keeps us in servitude. They twist the Holy Scriptures around to claim that the Bible says black people are descendents of Ham, who was cursed of God. The Bible clearly does not say this. The book of Genesis, chapter 9, verses 18–25 describes how one of Noah's three sons, Ham, did a disgraceful thing to his father. As a result, a curse was placed on *his son*, Canaan.

> Noah's curse, however, wasn't directed toward any particular race, but rather at the Canaanite nation—a nation God knew would become wicked. The curse *was fulfilled* [emphasis mine] when the Israelites entered the Promised Land and drove the Canaanites out (see the book of Joshua)[23]

There is not even any indication that the Canaanites were dark-skinned people.

Now that we have explored what the root cause is not, let us look at what truly drove men to perpetuate this bad episode. As mentioned already in the introduction to this chapter, the true spiritual root of this issue is pride.

> [Pride] is purely spiritual: consequently it is far more subtle and deadly [than other sins].[24]—C.S. Lewis

The sins that we can relate directly to physical consequences are easy to identify. For example, if a person kills someone, we can all see the physical evidence that a trespass has occurred. Pride is a little harder to identify; therefore, it can escalate unregulated and undetected to great proportions. This is what happened with the enslavement of African people and the growth of racism.

Pride drove African kings to sell subjects and conquered foes in order to have more precious and coveted things than neighboring nations. The competitive nature of pride drove European slave merchants to purchase more slaves than the next, to try to get the best bargains on human life, to try to sell human life to the highest bidders. Pride drove American slave owners to desire more slaves, more profit from his slaves, and to get more obedience from his slaves than his neighbor. The lure of feeling superior drove slave owners to fight to keep people in bondage long after it was economically advantageous. In general, competitive pride drove many men and women to desire more profit than the next person from the human suffering and degradation called American slavery.

On the surface it appears to be greed, but in reality it is pride disguised as greed.

> Greed may drive men into competition if there is not enough to go around; but the proud man, even when he has got more than he can possibly want, will try to get still more just to assert his power.[25]—C.S. Lewis

Because the pride drove the greed, it can almost be described with a new compound word: pridegreed. These two monsters interlocked, but pride was the instigator.

So there we have it then. The culprit is exposed. How does this help us? Well—it shows how it is more important to identify the spirit of the sin than the vessel through which that sin was manifested. That, in turn, helps us to see how this spirit is still at the very core of racism today. It is key in helping us to turn from this sin and heal. It is also important to know how and when this spirit of racism, spurred by pride, came into existence. Pride has been around since the fall of man, so we are not trying to identify when pride came into existence, but rather that pride is in fact the motivation. Knowing the details of the origin of the pride of racism reinforces the fact that racism did not always exists and inspires hope that it can be gotten rid of.

Upon examining the root of racism more closely, we see a complex entanglement of people, places, and periods. It is a combination of African pridegreed, European pridegreed, and American pridegreed (meaning all of the Americas and Caribbean Islands). What I found in my research is that there is relatively scarce documentation written by the actual participants on this monumental historical event. The slave trade is like a crime scene wiped clean. The European accounts of slave journeys are full of empirical data, skeletal information. They are very business-like and inhumane.[26] The African accounts are very rare and are narrowly focused on individual experiences, not on larger issues. One book, *Africa Remembered*, which compiled all the known legitimate records by slaves who experienced the Middle Passage shows only nine written accounts.[27] Nine written accounts from over 11 million people who suffered through the Middle Passage! Was this sin so egregious that men were compelled to refrain from recording it? Perhaps they thought not writing about it would somehow make it fade away. But truth is persistent and always comes out eventually.

How then can one group of people treat another peoples this badly without there being some natural, ingrained aversion? Well, simply put, if this hatred was not inbred, then it was instilled and there was a point of its actualization. When one has trespassed against another the easiest way to ease the conscience is to blame the victim. Then the guilty party rationalizes that because this victim bought this upon himself, they have the right to treat him any way they want as punishment for being the deserving victim. It becomes a vicious cycle. At what point did the hatred between European and African, white-skinned and brown-skinned people, crystallize? In his eye-opening book, *The Diligent*, historian Robert Harms gives compelling documentation of this as he describes how Europeans politely bartered with Africans for human lives during their stay in Africa, but quickly changed perspective once the ships set sail.

The Africans began to hate for obvious reasons. The whites feared mutiny and began to hate and fear their victims. In other words, the Middle Passage was the fermenting ground for racial hatred, fear, and hostility. Slave ships were floating incubators for racism in its infancy.[28]

Here is where the fear factor originated. This same us against them, blacks against whites, kill or be killed, mentality still haunts us today. This thinking says the battle is one culture against the other and that one's survival is predicated on the other's demise. Who is right? Who will win in the end? These questions continue to plague many modern minds.

Again, the slave trade was a complex mixture of sin and un-righteousness on the part of various groups of people over a long expanse of time. The three main categories I would like to ex-amine here are Africans, Europeans, and Americans. What are those things that pricked the pridegreed of so many Africans to make them to participate in such a detrimental trading? Many were lusting after European exported goods. Cowry shells, which came from India by way of Europe, were commonly used for currency in African nations.[29] These were as good as cash is for us today. Other European imports were coveted: cloth from the Dutch and India, cotton cloth, silk, iron beads, silver, tobacco, earthenware, and liquors.

Another indication of African pridegreed is the wars and ter-ritorial disputes which broke out over which African ruler would control certain ports. For example, the English fort at Whydah was fought over by the King of Whydah, King Assou, the Da-homey people led by King Agaja, and the Oyo peoples.[30] Also, the rise of the Asante Empire in the 1720's had a dramatic affect on the trade routes from the interior of Africa to the coast. The Asante essentially built up their military might by buying guns and gunpowder from the Dutch, then choked off the countries on the interior from trading goods on the coast. A complexity of wars arose that resulted in Asante people being sold into slavery as opposed to the goods from the interior being sold. This war-fare ultimately resulted in the gold coast's transformation into the slave coast.[31] The Owu war in the1820's also had a tremendous destabilizing affect on the region that lasted for many decades thereafter.[32]

Olaudah Equiano, a survivor of the Middle Passage who was kidnapped and sold into slavery in 1756, describes the situation eloquently:

> When a trader wants slaves, he applies to a chief for them, and tempts him with his wares. It is not extraordinary, if on this occasion he [the African] yields to the temptation with as little firmness, and accepts the price of his fellow creature's liberty with as little reluctance, as the enlightened merchant. Accordingly, he falls on his neighbours, and a desperate battle ensues.[33]

There is a tendency in our time to think mainly of Africans as the victims of slavery and Europeans and Americans mainly as the perpetrators. There is also the notion that at some point, the Africans got in too deep, so to speak, and could not stop the insatiable demand for their lives. Therefore, they were soon faced with a situation of sell your neighbor before he sells you. There may be an inkling of truth to this notion. The African soldiers of Whydah, during the early 1730's would often retreat from battles quickly because they feared being sold into slavery more than death even.[34] The many African wars related to the slave trade and the instability and turmoil that resulted could be used as evidence to support this theory.

Even so, this does not excuse the role that many Africans played in selling their fellowman or absolve them from the sin of pridegreed. And it does not erase the fact that many profited greatly and were spurred on to more avarice by their own lusts as opposed to by the fear of victimization. Take for example King Agaja, who reigned over the African country Dahomey during the 1720's. He had eleven palaces lavishly furnished with European goods that were obtained by trading slaves.[35] He terrorized neighboring African countries with his highly militarized army. They were well equipped with flintlock muskets, cannons, and gunpowder supplied by European traders. Agaja was the worst kind of tyrannical dictator. He is said to have had a collection of the skulls of men he conquered set in his palaces "'as thick as they can lie one by the other'"[36] His military regime relied not only on being well-trained and well-armed, but also on this type of psychological warfare that instilled fear in the hearts of his enemies.

> According to the tradition, King Huffon of Whydah [slave port] sent King Agaja a gift of forty lengths of cloth, forty barrels of gunpowder, forty muskets, forty bottles of rum, and forty cabesse of cowry shells (one cabesse equaled four thousand cowries). He taunted Agaja, asking if he was wealthy enough to give such an expensive gift without demanding anything in return. In response, King Agaja ordered his prime minister to prepare a path lined with two parallel rows of skulls of defeated enemies. He marched the emissaries of the king of Whydah along that grisly path and then gave each one a mere forty cowry shells.[37]

This same king, Agaja, when he found out why the whites demanded so many black slaves desired to start his own rival sugar plantations in Africa run by slave labor.[38]

King Huffon, ruler of the kingdom of Whydah, a very popular slave port in the early 1700's, also was a great benefactor of the slave trade. He is reported also to have led a decadent lifestyle and, judging from his gift challenge described in the above quote, he had an overabundance of goods to spare. His might was not military as Agaja's was, but was based on his diplomacy and skill in business dealings. Apparently, he buttered his bread on both sides. Not only did he get a thousand cowrie shells from Africans wanting to sell slaves from his port, but he also collected customs payments from the Europeans estimated to be worth twenty slaves for each vessel that landed at Whydah.[39]

Thus we cannot deduce that Africans in general were innocent victims of the Atlantic slave trade. We also cannot say that Africans were entirely ignorant of the consequences of being enslaved by the Europeans. But because much of African history at this time relied on oral tradition, this awareness and its extensiveness cannot be verified. However, we can deduce that initially, at least, there was no concern for the growing disdain by Europeans of dark-skinned people in general. There was no sense of unity between African peoples, nor should there have been. Each man saw himself as a citizen of his own nation, not an African. And even though the white men may have been feared as strange, unknown, and evil, there was no sense of uniting against them for the common black man's future well-being. "The sale by any ruler of a person of his own people would have been looked on as a severe punishment; when African kings or others sold prisoners of war, they looked on the persons concerned as aliens, about whose destiny they did not care, and who they might hate. For there was no sense of kinship between different African peoples."[40] Neither was there any sense of unity among European peoples. Although from many people's perspective today, the world is divided into black and white, it was not so back then because this type of division was just in its infancy. This was the time before racism.

The fact that Africans were culprits as well as victims in the slave trade is not widely   known. Contrastingly, it is a very well accepted fact that Europeans gained greatly in terms of worldly possessions. Again, it was their pride, coupled with greed that spurned them on. As we have already seen in the timeline, this monstrous transgression did not burst all at once into the history of man. Instead, the Mid-Atlantic slave trade started small, grew to a crescendo, then was gradually outlawed. Here are some highlights. The intent here is by no means to summarize comprehensively the history of the slave trade, but rather to point out illustrative incidences of where Satan got men to bite the bate of their own pride.

Basically, the Portuguese were the first to succumb. They initially raided African villages and kidnapped people for slaves. Historian Gomes Eannes de Zurara describes some of the Portuguese's first expeditions and one of the early records of cruelty in the capture of African slaves:

> Our men had very great toil in the capture of those who were swimming, for they dived like cormorants, so that they could not get hold of them; and the capture of the second man

caused them to lose all the others. For he was so valiant that two men, strong as they were, could not drag him into the boat until they took a boathook and caught him above one eye, and the pain of this made him abate his courage, and allow himself to be put into the boat.[41]

But soon the Portuguese found their desires could be more easily met by openly buying slaves and gold in the African markets, so they turned to a more diplomatic approach. The result was no less vile. In a relatively short time they had negotiated treaties with African rulers to purchase slaves in large quantities.

Initially, gold was the main draw tempting Portuguese explorers to venture further and further down the west coast of Africa. Many European countries had adopted gold as their currency in the eleventh and twelfth centuries. The original allure of the gold turned into the demand for human lives. There are a number of catalysts that contributed to that increase in slave trading. They are: 1) the European advances in ship building technology, 2) their advances in fort building technology, 3) advances in gun technology and production, 4) the rise of the sugar cane industry, 5) the decimation of the indigenous peoples of the Americas and the Caribbean, and 6) various decrees, laws, and ordinances put in place by European rulers and leaders. These events unfolded over centuries and in places so far apart from each other both physically and culturally that while they were happening they may have seemed unrelated. Some did not even seem noteworthy in and of themselves when they occurred. However, they are ominously interwoven into the picture we see today of the mid Atlantic slave trade.[42]

Looking at the various decisions that European leaders made concerning the slave trade, we see that their intentions were all to bolster their own economies. There is no record as to whether they gave any thought at all to the people whose lives would be destroyed. Prince Henry of Portugal, often called Prince Henry the Navigator, financed expeditions in the 1440's to explore the coast of Africa looking for gold and slaves. He was also interested in the Atlantic islands as speculative prospects for gaining wealth.[43] When King Ferdinand of Spain gave the order in 1510 that 200 African slaves be sent to the "new world" from Europe to mine gold in Hispaniola that marked the start of the slave traffic across the Atlantic.[44] Did he know what a floodgate he was opening? Probably not, but his mind was set on getting free labor to get himself more gold. King John III (Joao III) of Portugal also set another milestone in place when he gave permission for slave ships to go directly from Africa to the Americas in the 1530's. The 360 licenses the King gave to import slaves to Peru from Africa fueled a great boom in the slave trade.[45]

All of the maritime nations of Europe at some point had some government-sponsored involvement in the slave trade through trading companies and/or taxation of private traders. The Portuguese had the Cacheu Company, the Maranhao and Pernambuco Companies. Holland sponsored the infamous West India Company while Britain had the well-known Royal African Company and the South Sea Company. Spain had many different companies. The French worked through various Guinea companies and even the Scandinavian countries were involved.[46] These nations, "divided though they might be on every other matter, had a mutual interest in the prosperity of the slave traffic . . . [and] sought to establish numbers of slaves to be carried, as well as the prices at which they were to be sold. . . . Only the Portuguese tried to . . . lay down rules how the slaves were to be treated and transported."[47]

Not only were national economies greatly bolstered by slavery, but individuals amassed a large amount of ill-gotten gain in this way as well. One of many notable example is Richard Oswald, a Scottish-born citizen of Britain, who had property all over the world financed by his dealings in human bondage. He owned a share in Bence Island, a slave port off the coast of Sierra Leone. Although I have no direct description of the slave prisons at Bence in particular, slave ports were notorious for their squalid conditions. For example, the British owned Cape Coast castle was carved out of the rock below an existing castle, making it a literal dungeon. The number of slaves that died because of horrific conditions was so remarkably that it almost caused the English to renovate.[48] This was not for the sake of humanity, but to protect profits. In sharp contrast to these grisly conditions is the imagery of Richard Oswald playing rounds of golf with slave ship captains on the Bence Island golf course. He built the course on the fort to keep the captains entertained while they awaited their human cargo.[49] They also enjoyed a "luxurious central building with 'a very cool and convenient gallery.'"[50] Meanwhile, the African captives suffered unthinkable conditions in the dungeons below. Oswald made so much blood money that he was able to retire in the comfort and excesses of his palace at Auchincruive in Scotland.[51] He is just one of many Europeans who built their personal fortunes on the backs of enslaved Africans.

European nations battled for control of slave forts in the same way that Africans did. Whoever controlled the fort, received the most levies. But that did not stop greedy Europeans from patronizing opposing nation's forts because the demand for slaves was so ridiculously inflated. In assessing the great gathering of ships awaiting slave cargo at Whydah in 1728, the fort director commented "that perhaps the real problem was too many ships instead of too few slaves."[52]

The French port city of Nantes was built on the backs of slaves. Fifty-five percent of the French slave voyages originated there. It was a city characterized by its "opulent new mansions, its new mercantile exchange, and its opera house." This city became the standard to which other slave ports in France aspired.[53] This is a great example of how competitive zeal and hometown pride contributed to the decimation of millions of lives.

On the other side of the Atlantic we see American pride-greed. The descriptions of daily life that were highlighted in the previous chapter demonstrate the level of atrocity of the oppression black people suffered in order for this nation to profit.

It is noteworthy that the heyday (or more accurately said, "low" day) of the slave trade coincides with the discriminatory laws being enacted in America. [See timeline illustration]. After Americans discovered that people with a great deal of melanin in their skin could be easily identified and set apart from people with little melanin, they took the diabolical bait and legislated that the former should be decreed slaves for life. We see on the timeline that the first Africans arrived in Jamestown, Virginia in 1619. This cargo must have included a very small number of slaves because by 1649 there were only three hundred black slaves recorded in Virginia.[54] White, black, and Indian slaves worked together until the discriminatory laws were passed.[55] By the mid 1770's there were as many blacks in Virginia as whites and in South Carolina the black population was double that of the white.[56]

The institution of slavery has often been labeled "peculiar." There was something always off-kilter about the reasoning and the arguments for sustaining and defending this institution. Where there is sin, there is also the natural tendency to denial. So it is quite peculiar that southerners who argued for slavery often denied that it was economically profitable to slave owners.[57] They would rather believe that people with little melanin in their skin were helping the darker skinned people by keeping them in this state that was more suited to them. Also, they propagated the myth that somehow all of this was meant to be, that is was the right order of things put into place by unstoppable cosmic forces. All the while slaves rebelled continuously against this state. Some of it was active, violent rebellion such as the slave uprisings led by Nat Turner. Most of it, however, was subtle, daily resistance such as working as slow and ineffectively as possible, feigning illnesses, scraping together meager lifetime savings to buy freedom, persistently petitioning owners for freedom for self and children, and constantly running away or attempting to escape.[58]

American slave owners never wanted to admit that it was their greed and pride that led them down this wrong path. The following passage sums up well the pride and jealously that drove greedy slave masters:

A stanch defender of slavery described a set of avaricious planters whom he labeled "Cotton Snobs," or "Southern Yankees." In their frantic quest for wealth, he wrote indignantly, the crack of the whip was heard early and late, until their bondsmen were "bowed to the ground with over-tasking and over-toil." A southern physician who practice on many cotton plantations complained, in 1847, that some masters still regarded "their sole interest to consist in large crops, leaving out of view altogether the value of negro property and its possible deterioration." . . . An Alabama newspaper attributed conditions such as these to "avarice, the desire of growing rich."[59]

From the following passage of scripture we see that God cares even about animals that are used for labor.

> For the scripture saith, thou shalt not muzzle the ox that treadeth out the corn. And, the labourer is worthy of his reward. (I Timothy 5:18)

How much more egregious a transgression then was it to subject His human creations, created in His image and likeness, to work without pay—for four hundred years? This is why the institution was always peculiar and never was normal or acceptable. Going against God's will is like swimming against the tide. It is always a struggle, and one with no worthy gain.

Even when slavery ceased to be economically profitable (right before the Civil War) pro-slavery southerners were determined to continue this aberrant way of life.[60] Why? Because now their pride was well puffed-up with the notion that they were inherently better than black people. No matter how bad things got for them, they always would have the slave to look down upon. This sentiment lingers today in a lot of the anger and opposition some whites have to black progress. Through slavery, the pride of whites was pricked with the notion of a permanent underclass. Another reason why the resistance was so staunch is because not only could whites feel superior to blacks, but also, they could control black slaves. According to C.S. Lewis, control is the power that pride enjoys.

> Power is what Pride really enjoys: there is nothing makes a man feel so superior to others as being able to move them about like toy soldiers.[61]

In conclusion, the root cause of slavery is that Satan, the father of lies, is an equal opportunity tempter. There were an estimated forty thousand slave voyages across the Atlantic that carried more than 11 million people to destruction.[62] Most times the only commonality between the people who gained was greed and competitive pride.[63] The devil will use anyone who is willing to succumb to his own pride. He caught Africans, Europeans, and Americans in their foolish pride and the results were and continue to be disastrous.

Chapter Three Endnotes

1. Clive Staples Lewis, *Mere Christianity*, (New York: Harper-Collins, 1952) 121.

2. Lewis, *Mere Christianity*, 122.

3. Lewis, *Mere Christianity* ,123.

4. Sanderson Beck, *Middle East and Africa to 1875*, quoted on the website www.san.beck.org/1-14-Africa1800-1875.html.

5. Robert Harms, *The Diligent: A Voyage Through the Worlds of the Slave Trade* (New York: Basic Books, 2002) 135–136.

6. Jennifer M. Payne, "Influences of British Imperialist Economic Fortunes on Slavery, Sugar, Abolition" (The Wedderburn Pages website, 1994) http://wedderburn.alpesprovence.net/slavhist.htm.

7. Thomas, *The Slave Trade*, 62.

8. Note: This research can be found in *They Came Before Columbus: The African Presence in Ancient America* by Ivan Van Sertima, (New York: Random House, Inc.,1976).

9. Phillip Curtin, *Africa Remembered: Narratives by West Africans from the Era of the Slave Trade*, (Prospect Heights, Il.: Waveland Press, Inc., 1997),70.

10. Thomas, *The Slave Trade*, 42.

11. Heroditus, Everyman's Library ed., 2 vols. (London: 1924) vol. 1, 220 quoted in Thomas, *The Slave Trade*, 27.

12. Fr. Martin de Cordoba, *Un jardin de las doncellas* (Valladolid, 1500), qu. Peggy Liss, *Isabel the Queen* (Oxford, 1992) 304, quoted in Thomas, *The Slave Trade*, 71.

13. Harms, *The Diligent*, 18.

14. Harms, *The Diligent*, 16.

15. Harms, *The Diligent*, 19–20.

16. Harms, *The Diligent*, 18.

17. Thomas, *The Slave Trade*, 25.

18. Thomas, *The Slave Trade*, 41.

19. Thomas, *The Slave Trade*, 112.

20. Harms, *The Diligent*, 147.

21. Harms, *The Diligent*, 122.

22. Harms, *The Diligent*, 121–123.

23. Various contributors, *Life Applications Study Bible*, Tyndale House Publishers, Wheaton, IL, 1988, 22–23.

24. Lewis, *Mere Christianity*, 125.
25. Lewis, *Mere Christianity*, 123.
26. Harms, *The Diligent*, 303.
27. Curtin, *Africa Remembered*.
28. Harms, *The Diligent*, 301.
29. Curtin, *Africa Remembered*, 270.
30. Harms, *The Diligent*, 213–217.
31. Harms, *The Diligent*, 135–136.
32. Curtin, *Africa Remembered*, 198.
33. Curtin, *Africa Remembered*, 77.
34. Harms, *The Diligent*, 171–172.
35. Harms, *The Diligent*, 169–173.
36. Harms, *The Diligent*, 173.
37. Harms, *The Diligent*, 173.
38. Harms, *The Diligent*, 175.
39. Harms, *The Diligent*, 153–155, 161.
40. Thomas, *The Slave Trade*, 59.
41. Zurara (Azurara)'s Chronicle of the Discovery of Guinea, Eng. tr. ed C. R. Beazley and Edgar Prestage, Hakluyt Society, 1st ser., vols. 95 and 100 (London, 1896 and 1899). Zurara, [1,1], 121 quoted in Thomas, *The Slave Trade*, 57.
42. Thomas, *The Slave Trade*, general.
43. Thomas, *The Slave Trade*, 52–57.
44. Thomas, *The Slave Trade*, 92–93.
45. Thomas, *The Slave Trade*, 102–103.
46. Thomas, *The Slave Trade*, 292.
47. Thomas, *The Slave Trade*, 292–293.
48. Harms, *The Diligent*, 140.
49. Thomas, *The Slave Trade*, 10.
50. Thomas, *The Slave Trade*, 342.
51. Thomas, *The Slave Trade*, 297.
52. Harms, *The Diligent*, 212.
53. Harms, *The Diligent*, xvii.
54. Stampp, *The Peculiar Institution*, 21.
55. Stampp, *The Peculiar Institution*, 21–24.
56. Stampp, *The Peculiar Institution*, 24.
57. Stampp, *The Peculiar Institution*, 383.
58. Stampp, *The Peculiar Institution*, 86, 140, chapter 3.

59. Stampp, *The Peculiar Institution,* 84–85.

60. Stampp, *The Peculiar Institution*, 384.

61. Lewis, *Mere Christianity*, 123.

62. Harms, *The Diligent*, xiv. Note: this figure is widely disputed mainly by people of African descent to be too low.

63. Harms, *The Diligent*, xx.

Chapter Four

Oh, What a Tangled Web!

Oh what a tangled web we weave, when first we practise to
deceive. —Sir Walter Scott

The seed of racism is slavery, which was rooted in greedy
pride. Having studied the root, the seed, and the crop, let us now
look more in depth at the growth of the plant. Racism had another growth spurt after the cancer of official slavery ended.
More specifically, there is an offshoot of racism that I call
pseudo-scientific racism. This phenomena was a shot in the arm
to a concept that was being successfully overcome at the turn of
the 19th century. What pseudo-scientific racism attempts to do is
to "prove" scientifically that white people are superior to blacks
thereby rendering the whole sin of slavery justified. These theories began to bud in the mid 19th century and sprang mainly
from the theory of evolution espoused by Charles Darwin. Before this theory was espoused, proponents of slavery misused the
Bible as their authority. The theory of evolution allowed men to
abandon the Biblical account of creation for this new "scientific"
evidence that "species" have evolved into what we see today.
The hidden racism in this thinking is that black and white people
are different "species" and that white people are in fact a more

highly-evolved "species" of people. That makes slavery and oppression of blacks by whites the natural order of things. Evolu-
tionary racism has created offshoots that are as tangled as a
mangled spider web. Once humanity started down the road of
pseudc-scientific racism, Satan took the reigns and started pull-
ing. He takes those who fall for this lie as far down as they will
go. The further down this darkened path they go, the more complex things get.

But the good news is that there is scientific evidence against
evolution. The even better news is that there is Biblical evidence
against evolution and against racism in general.

As mentioned in the second chapter, the spin-off sins from
slavery have been far-reaching and many. The "Tangled Web"
illustration on the next page shows how the Theory of Evolution
comes into the mix. Note that slavery is not the only sin leading
to these spin-offs, but it has had a great influence in these problems as they manifest in American society today. The African
holocaust is not the only prideful and greedy thing that has led to
downfall and chaos, but the focus here is to examine the ties that
it does have. Those particular bonds related to it will be broken
with healing from this sin.

In reviewing the diagram we see at the very top that Pride
led to greed that led to competition. Who can work his slaves the
"best?" Who can control his slaves "best?" Who can make his
slaves bow down the "best?" And finally, who has the most
slaves? One's worth and status, another driver in the competitive
greed that plagued the American slave owner, was measured also
by the number of slaves he owned.

And so the slave trade did escalate as illustrated in the diagram. This led to the dehumanization of Africans and their inhumane treatment in order to ensure profit. In order to treat
someone so cruelly, the white captors had to harden their hearts.
In turn there was a backlash of hatred and fear in the hearts of
the black captives. Here is a testimony and an example told from
a slave who went through the Middle Passage:

Figure 4.1 Tangled Web Illustration
Note: these are the author's
original thoughts.

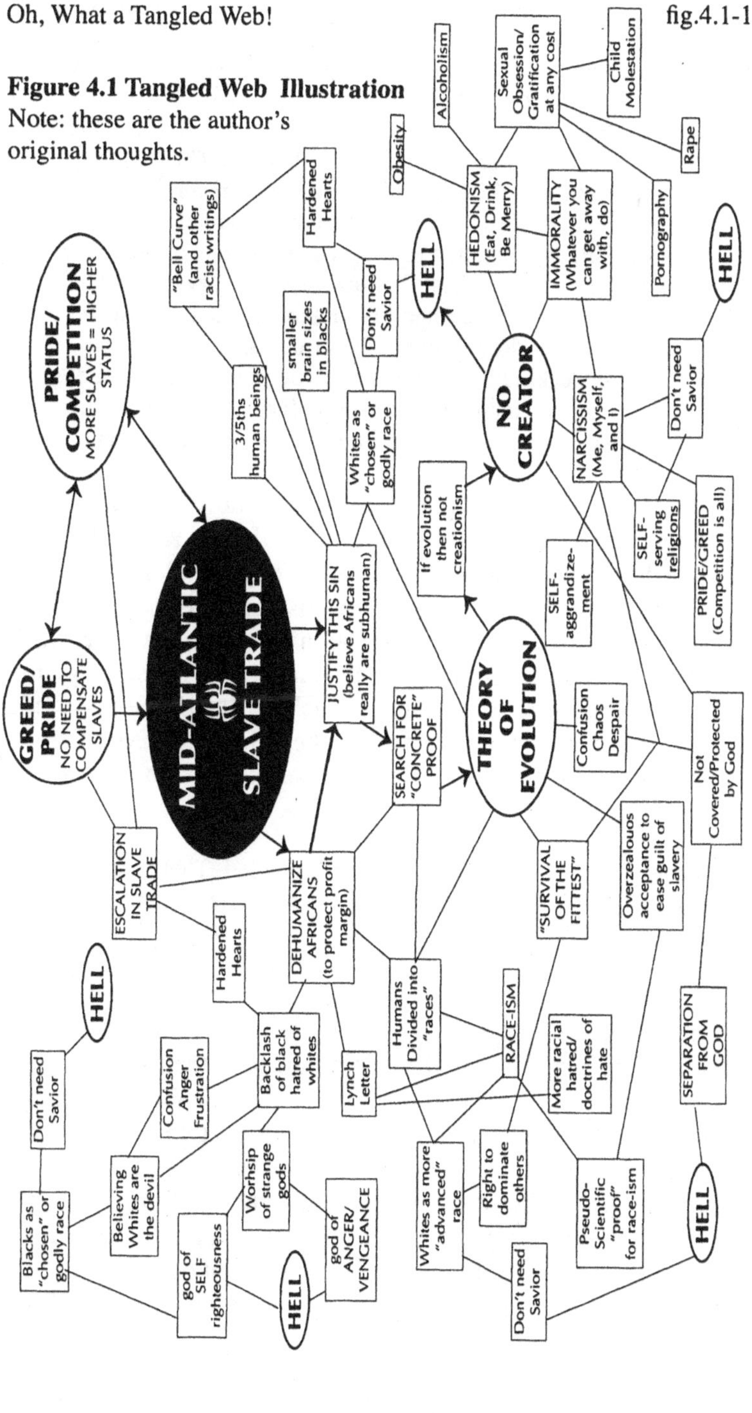

For I had never seen among any people such instances of brutal cruelty; and this not only towards us blacks, but also to
some of the whites themselves. . . . We were all put under
deck, . . . it became absolutely pestilential. . . . The groans of
the dying, rendered the scene of horror almost inconceivable. .
. . Every circumstance I met with served only to render my state
more painful, and heighten my apprehensions and my opinion
of the cruelty of the whites. One day they had taken a number
of fishes; and when they had killed and satisfied themselves
with as much as they thought fit, to our astonishment who
were on the deck, rather than give any of them to us to eat, as
we expected, they tossed the remaining fish into the sea again,
although we begged and prayed for some.—Olaudah Equiano[1]

This is one clear example of cruelty, but no one wants to see
himself as a greedy, hard-hearted torturer. Here is where the justification by pseudo-science becomes so tempting to those bound
by the sin of racism. The research can easily be misunderstood as
"proof" that people with more melanin are subhuman, i.e. that
blacks are essentially "less evolved" than whites. In the diagram
we see the jump from the "Slave Trade" to "justifying this sin"
to "the search for 'concrete' proof" to the "Theory of Evolution."
    That web leads to the web that says there is no creator, a
foolish notion, indeed!

The fool hath said in his heart, there is no God. They are corrupt, they have done abominable works, there is none that
doeth good. (Psalm 14:1)

The theory of evolution says there is no creator. That we are
just meaningless accidental occurrences in a universe that
evolved of nothingness. If there is no creator, then there is no
God. If there is no God, then there is no accountability. Therefore why not do whatever you want? Why not let yourself be led
by your animal instincts? Whatever feels good to you is good.
This is hedonism. Thus the lines in the diagram go from "Theory
of Evolution" to "No Creator." Evolution says each man for
himself; never mind your fellowman. It is all about survival of
the fittest and rugged individualism. This is narcissism. All of it

is foolishness to God and, as we see in the connections on the diagram, ultimately leads souls directly to hell.

Now the paradox about the theory of Evolution is that although it leads people to believe there is no supernatural God, it does lead to the thinking that white people are a "godly" race by reason of the fact that they are more "evolved" than blacks. Should not they be more respected, more privileged? This tangles back into the pride that spurns the greed that begets the hatred/envy that leads to hell. Intertwined with that is the backlash of anger and resentment eating away at many black people. Consuming anger leads to self-pity, or self-righteousness, or vengeance, or any combination thereof. This backlash has contributed to the thinking that white people are the devil. If white people are the devil, then blacks, being their opposites, must therefore be the chosen, or "godly" race. This tangles back into the pride that spurns the greed that begets the hatred/envy that leads to hell. In summary you will notice in the illustration that all of the ends of the web lead to hell. Belief in evolution leads to hell.

Darwinism and its spawn is a milestone for the enemy in the battle against the sin of racism; therefore, special investigation of this phenomena is warranted. I found that pseudo-science, with its sterile numbers, abstract theories and analyses appears at first blush to be quite high-minded and intelligent. This facade makes exposing its low-down dirtiness very challenging. It was exhausting and painful just reading about the cast of characters and their "research" and trying to follow their flawed and evil logic. It is important, however, to review it in order to expose the enemy's deception. Another benefit is that it reveals the stark contrast between Satan's dark deception about people verses God's marvelous view and plan.

Let us begin with the founder, Charles Darwin. In his landmark biological study, he observed that species seemed to adapt to their environment. He assumed this adaptation is an advancement of species by a process that he labeled "natural selection." His well-known book, *The Origins of Species by means of Natural Selection or the Preservation of the Favoured Races in the Struggle for Life* was published in 1859. Many of his followers deny that his intentions in these writings were racists. They paint him as an innocent theorist who simply documented what he observed in nature. They claim that others took his theory and misused it on human "races." However, as the authors of the book *One Blood: The Biblical Answer to Racism* point out, the subtitle of the book speaks for itself.[2]

> Darwinism spawned the belief that some races were physically closer to the lower primates and were also inferior. The polyphyletic view was that blacks evolved from the strong but less intelligent gorillas, the Orientals from the Orangutans, and whites form the most intelligent of all primates, the chimpanzees. The belief that blacks were less evolved than whites, and (as many early evolutionists concluded) that they would eventually become extinct, is a major chapter in Darwinism history. The nefarious fruits of evolutionism, from the Nazis' conception of racial superiority to its utilization in developing their governmental policy, are all well documented.[3]

Not so well documented are the hopes of American pseudoscience supporters who also hoped that blacks would become extinct.

> Each new American census showed that this prediction of Darwin was wrong because "the black population showed no signs of failing, and might even be on the rise." Not content "to wait for natural selection to grind out the answer," one senator even tried to establish programs to convince—or even force—Afro-Americans to return to Africa.[4]

Ham, Weiland, and Batten, the authors of *One Blood*, also found documentation of Darwin directly espousing racism.

> On the last page of his book *The Descent of Man*, Darwin expressed the opinion that he would rather be descended from a monkey than from a "savage." He used the words savage, low, and degraded to describe the American Indians, the Andaman Island Pygmies, and the representatives of almost every ethnic group whose physical appearance and culture differed from his own. . . . [In this way] Charles Darwin labeled "the

low and degraded inhabitants of the Andaman Islands." . . .
The Iruri Forest Pygmies have been compared to "lower organisms."[5]

These are not the thoughts of a man innocent of racial bias.
Charles Darwin did in fact clearly spew racism.

After Darwin a man named Earnest Haeckel (1834–1919)
took the reigns. Haeckel theorized that all creation is on a pro-
gression to a higher order. Therefore, the reverse must be true,
i.e. that we cam from a lower order and ultimately must have
started from the lowest order. He taught that humans evolved
from apes but that ultimately everything had evolved from a sin-
gle-cell organism. Haeckel's mission in life was to find the
"missing link" between primates and humans.[6] He preached that
nature was god. In his writings of 1899 he touted nature as the
new religion.[7] Haeckel worked together with a man named
Weisman to promote Rassenhygeine, a term coined by Alfred
Ploetz, which translated means racial hygiene. Rassenhygeine is
defined as "the careful and planned improvement of the race."
These men's dangerous thoughts had a huge influence on the
German Nazi party.[8]

The lie to be exposed here is that we evolved from primates,
who evolved from amoeba. Therefore, we are just a natural part
of the environment. Since we see in nature organisms overtaking
other organisms, certain plants choking out other plant life, animals and their prey, then our human relationships naturally follow the same course. I call this the dog-eat-dog worldview. Eat
or be eaten. In fact, evolutionism tells us to feel free to act on all
of our "animal" instincts. It is only natural to do what feels good
to you. This is contrary to God's word firstly because He gave
man dominion *over* the things of the earth. Secondly, man is a
much higher order of creation than plants and animals. We have
a unique consciousness. Unlike other creatures, God created us
in his image and likeness.

And God blessed them, and God said unto them, Be fruitful,
and multiply, and replenish the earth, and subdue it: and have
dominion over the fish of the sea, and over the fowl of the air,

and over every living thing that moveth upon the earth. (Genesis 1:28)

Haeckel's contemporaries in this movement applied the well-known term, "survival of the fittest" to their erroneous thought patterns. They also expanded it by hypothesizing that humans have evolved at different rates in different environments, which accounts for some races being more highly "evolved" than others.[9] The next offshoot was an idea called eugenics, which I define as helping the "fittest" out-survive the "unfit" more speedily by actively eliminating the "unfit." This idea flourished around 1883 and was promoted by a man named Frances Galton.[10] Galton and his successors also promoted "laissez-faire" government, which meant that the government should not help the "unfit" (read the poor, the oppressed) because they are destined to extinction anyway.[11] Because these scientists do not know God, the true Creator of heaven and earth, they also do not believe in the devil. Therefore, they are easily blinded and blindsided by his deception. The foundation of all their work is a lie. Charles Darwin's seemingly simple observation that species adapt to their environment snowballed here into unadulterated racism. This tangled and twisted logic has continued to feed on itself with ominous consequences.

The next milestone in the evolution of racism was the categorization of human beings. Two men, Carleton Coon (1904–1981) and William H. Sheldon (1898–1997) led the charge postulating that people are all of one of the following: caucasoids, negroids, mongoloids, austaloids, or capoids.[12] These categories furthered the thinking that people groups are vastly distinct and can easily and obviously be grouped into these various categories. Sheldon's work also claimed to prove that behavioral traits, such as criminality, are genetically determined.[13] They believed themselves to be in search of the "truth" no matter what the consequences. Whatever "Mother Nature" should tell them through their microscopes they trusted would be the "truth." They claimed not to be racist, only "pure" theorists. Ironically, they studied their work laboriously and meticulously, yet claim dumb innocence of the history and impact of enslavement and oppression of African people. They and others like them seem shocked and surprised when they are accused of racism or when their "research" is used by racists. By keeping their heads in books and their eyes on charts and graphs they manage to virtually ignore the dragon in the room, racism. They worship creation and give no thought to the Creator. No thought is given as to the One who gave them the ability to think all of their so-called high-minded thoughts. No thought is given to things spiritual, only analytical things.

Some scientists tried to combat these racist theories by saying that environment plays a major role in determining a persons level of success or "fitness" in the world. In their eyes the battle of life is over what determines human behavior: biological factors verses environment. The true and ultimate battle however is good against evil. These behavioral proponents tried also to use empirical data to prove that humans could not be grouped into "races." However, without any spiritual understanding of just how dangerous mis-categorization is in the first place, they had no authority. I liken it to trying to slay the dragon in the room, but blindfolded and with a butter knife. First the spiritual depravation of evolutionism must be exposed in order to effectively challenge its conclusions.

> For we wrestle not against flesh and blood, but against principalities, against powers, against the rulers of the darkness of this world, against spiritual wickedness in high places. (Ephesians 6:12)

The scientific racism movement did not end in the middle of the 20th century, but thrives on today. For example there is the controversial Human Genome Project, begun in the 1980's, which aims to use the map of the human genome to determine genetic markers for various traits.[14] Some of its research involves isolating genes for "impulsiveness" (read criminality).[15] The theory is that genes predetermine what people will do and who they will be. Morality and choice play no part. Similar to that is the recent Federal Violence Initiative. The "Violence Initiative" is a conglomerate of over 300 research projects "focusing on screening out and treating preventively violence prone individuals" based on studies of early behavior and biological markers.[16] The person initially slated to head this effort, Dr. Frederick Goodwin, resigned in a cloud of controversy. He allegedly made racist remarks saying that black youths only had primal urges to kill, have sex, and procreate. This initiative hearkens back to its evil predecessor, "laissez-faire" government. The United States government would "help" the people who are out of control genetically, the ones who just cannot help becoming the criminals that they are. This "help" would come by means of by numbing them with drugs and dumbing down their educational opportunities at an early age. Many in the African American community were outraged at the tone and the implications of this initiative and organized opposition. Once again, however, I do not see that any spiritual authority was invoked in the battle.

This is just a cursory glance at the web of pseudo-scientific racism. The irony of the whole movement is that there is sound scientific evidence against racism. Even though we should not rely on science to give us truth, we can use it as an instrument to demonstrate absolute truth. Scientists who have studied this issue biologically admit that there is only one human "race"—homo sapiens.[17] There are only slight differences in our physical attributes. They may seem like glaring differences outwardly, but are only minor in reality. Take skin color for example. It may seem like there are white-skinned people and brown-skinned people and a host of others in between. However, I have known some black people who had lighter skin than many white people. On the other hand I have seen some Italian and Greek white people who have a very dark coloring. A person's coloring is only dependent on the amount of melanin in his or her skin. It is simply a chemical/biological differing in quantities.[18]

The authors of *One Blood* go on to explain that all of our other features can be analyzed similarly. "No people group has anything that is, in its essence, uniquely different from that possessed by another."[19] They use the Asian eye as another example, explaining that Asian people simply have more fat in the upper eyelids than most whites and therefore their eyes may appear more closed.[20] They then go on to make a profound analysis of hereditary combinations. One example we see today is tightly curled hair and dark skin. They conclude that the combinations we have now are only the result of social and environmental barriers and could potentially be very different if those barriers were removed.[21]

In essence, Satan has deceived many into believing that humans are divided into "races," limited to the people group characteristics we see now, and that some groups are inherently better than others.

The Bible teaches the exact opposite:

> And Adam called his wife's name Eve; because she was the mother of all living. (Genesis 3:20)

Even genetic researchers have had their eyes opened to this truth that God has plainly stated: we are all descendents of Eve. Therefore we are all descendents of Adam and Eve. Researchers at the University of California, Berkeley did a groundbreaking study on the ancestry of the human race. Because of breakthroughs in understanding DNA they now know that there is a particular type called mitochondrial DNA (mtDNA) that is only inherited maternally. In other words, your father does not contribute at all to this gene because his does not combine with your mother's to make yours. They took a sampling of mtDNA and, using computer modeling, were able to create a family tree of the human race by tracing the genes back maternally. In conclusion they said, "We can therefore view the tree as a genealogy linking maternal lineages in modern human populations to a common ancestral female."[22] They also indicated that this woman was African; therefore, when the press reported this information it was sensationalized as the "African Eve" story. Not only did the research indicate that we are all of one blood, but it also invalidates the idea that "races" evolved separately.

Scientists have also actually disproved the theory of evolution statistically. The landmark experiment for evolutionists occurred back in 1953. A scientist named Stanley Miller claimed he had created a model of the earth's early atmosphere. In his created biosphere he simulated lightening and its effects and claimed that it caused amino acids (or life) to form. His study was based on the assumption that the earth's atmosphere was initially composed of very volatile gases. However, in 1980 scientists at NASA disproved this assumption and found that in fact the opposite was true. The earth's atmosphere was made of very inert gases from its inception and has not changed much since.[23] Under these conditions, scientists have concluded, "The odds of [accidentally] creating just one functional protein molecule would be one chance in a 10 with 60 zeroes after it."[24] "Sir Frederick Hoyle put it artfully when he said that 'this scenario is as likely as a tornado whirling through a junkyard and accidentally assembling a fully functional Boeing 747.'"[25] I highly recommend reading the book, *The Case for Faith*, for further explanation not only of this issue, but also of many questions people have about the Christian faith.

Even more important than the scientific evidence against racism and evolution is the Biblical evidence. It begins in the very first book and the very first chapter of the Bible. Then from Genesis to Revelation we learn that all of us are the same: sinners who need salvation.

> And God said, Let us make man in our image, after our likeness: and let them have dominion over the fish of the sea, and over the fowl of the air, and over the cattle, and over all the earth, and over every creeping thing that creepeth upon the earth. So God created man in his own image, in the image of God created he him; male and female created he them. (Genesis 1: 26–27)

So God made us, all of us, in His image and likeness. He then goes on to say in Genesis 1:31 that it was very good [emphasis mine]. Evolutionists want you to believe that you are a random accident that grew out of an amoeba. Eventually you will go back to be dust in the earth when you die, but all this is for no particular reason except to fertilize the grass. It is a very sad way of thinking, especially when compared to the Biblical view, which tells us we are a reflection of the creator of the universe! That knowledge made King David give God even more praise.

I will praise thee; for I am fearfully and wonderfully made: marvelous are thy works; and that my soul knoweth right well. (Psalm 139:14)

The hurt and pain of racism in my own life prevented me from appreciating this about God for a very long time. As a child I felt that my nose was too wide, my lips were too big, and my hair was too nappy. I was envious of my white friends who had long straight hair. I used to hope that God would change me, especially my hair. I was not born with these feelings of inferiority. They were instilled in me by this culture and by the notion that my "race" was inherently inferior to that of others. When relaxers (products to straighten black hair) became popular, I pleaded with my mother to have one. Because she wore her hair in a natural afro, she was quite opposed to the idea. Finally she gave in. It was not until after graduate school that I mustered the courage to let my hair grow in its natural state again. It was more common in the 1960's when my mother was a young woman for black women to wear "naturals," and the trend is making a comeback today. However, when I first began, very few of us wore it this way. That is why I see it as an act of courage and a statement of faith. I have come to understand that it is God who made my hair and all my other features the way they are. It must be pleasing in His sight. I am able to praise Him, knowing this in my soul. Coming to faith in Christ Jesus has made me appreciate this even more. Now I know that it is man who judges people by outward appearances. God looks at the inner man—the soul, the heart, the motivation.

The Bible tells us that God made us all of one blood.

And [He] hath made of one blood all nations of men for to dwell on all the face of the earth. (Acts 17:26a)

We are all physical descendants from Adam and Eve. Not only that, but they are also our spiritual ancestors. We are all born into sin and with a sin nature because they decided to sin against God. When they did, sin and death entered into the world (Romans 5:12).

According to the God's word, man's "truths" cannot be trusted.

> The heart is deceitful above all things, and desperately wicked: who can know it? (Jeremiah 17:9)

In desperate wickedness man has tried to categorize and divide people by physical features and cultures in order to oppress and exploit some while exalting others. According to Biblical history, God divided people into different cultures at the tower of Babel (Genesis 11:8–9).[26] The people wanted to exalt themselves to be as high as God so he "confounded the language" and "scattered them abroad upon the face of all the earth." The people were all being equally evil and thus the scattering.

Moving further along in the Bible we see that God chooses the nation of Israel to be His people. This was God's sovereign choice and had nothing to do with these people being better than any other people. They fell into slavery at the hands of Egyptians. When they cried unto God for help, God heard their pleas with compassion.

> And it came to pass in process of time, that the king of Egypt died: and the children of Israel sighed by reason of the bondage, and they cried, and their cry came up unto God by reason of the bondage. And God heard their groaning. (Exodus 2:23–24a)

Most people are familiar with the account of how God miraculously brought them up out of slavery in Egypt. Once the people were free, God instituted laws to govern them. Included therein we see that the Lord decreed fairness to workers, which indicates He certainly was against slavery.

> Thou shalt not defraud thy neighbour, neither rob him: the wages of him that is hired shall not abide with thee all night until the morning. (Leviticus 19:13)

In this passage God says that it is fraud even to hold workers wages overnight. He should be paid for his day's work on that very same day that the work is done.

In another passage God denounces oppression of workers in general, even non-Israelites.

> Thou shalt not oppress an hired servant that is poor and needy, whether he be of thy brethren, or of thy strangers that are in thy land within thy gates: (Deuteronomy 24:14–15)

Further along in the Old Testament of the Bible the prophet Jeremiah, who was God's mouthpiece, warns against the consequences of practicing slavery.

> Woe unto him that buildeth his house by unrighteousness, and his chambers by wrong; that useth his neighbour's service without wages, and giveth him not for his work; (Jeremiah 22:13)

Even in the New Testament, God's stance remains the same.

> Behold, the hire of the labourers who have reaped down your fields, which is of you kept back by fraud, crieth: and the cries of them which have reaped are entered into the ears of the Lord of sabaoth. (James 5:4)

Old Testament people of God looked forward to the coming of the Messiah, the Savior. Jesus came here in the flesh. He bore all of our sins when He died on the cross. He was resurrected from the grave and ascended into to heaven. Jesus stands at the pinnacle of time and He is the great equalizer. We are all equally guilty and born with a sin nature. We are all equally hell bound without Christ. When He was crucified Jesus took on the punishment for all sins, the sins of every single person who ever lived, is living now, and will ever live. He gave us all equal access to salvation—thereby making us equal.

And he is the propitiation for our sins: and not for ours only,
but also for the sins of the whole world. (I John 2:2)

He did not discriminate when He committed this tremendous
act of love. He did it for all of the different ethnic and cultural
groups in the world.

For thou wast slain, and hast redeemed us to God by thy blood
out of every kindred, and tongue, and people, and nation:
(Revelation 5:9)

When He commanded His disciples to go out, he said to
make disciples of "all nations." Thus this quote from the book
of Revelation reveals that every kind of people will be repre-
sented among those who have trusted Christ.

Furthermore God does not categorize his followers by race.
Everyone who has trusted Christ as Savior is one people.

There is neither Jew nor Greek, there is neither bond nor free,
there is neither male nor female: for ye are all one in Christ Jesus. (Galatians 3: 28)

He does divide humanity, however. His classifications have
nothing to do with outward appearance, culture, or ethnicity. He
separates all of humanity into sheep and goat, into those who are
His and those who are "none of His."

But ye [believers in Christ] are not in the flesh, but in the
Spirit, if so be that the Spirit of God dwell in you. Now if any
man have not the Spirit of Christ, he is none of his. (Romans
8:9)

When the Son of man shall come in his glory, and all the holy
angels with him, then shall he sit upon the throne of his
glory: And before him shall be gathered all nations: and he
shall separate them one from another, as a shepherd divideth
his sheep from the goats: And he shall set the sheep on his
right hand, but the goats on the left. Then shall the King say
unto them on his right hand, Come, ye blessed of my Father,

inherit the kingdom prepared for you from the foundation of
the world.
Then shall he say also unto them on the left hand, Depart from
me, ye cursed, into everlasting fire, prepared for the devil and
his angels: (Matthew 25:31–34, 41)

The devil and his angels really started something when they
pricked men's hearts with the greed for gain and the pride of
power that emanated from the Mid-Atlantic slave trade and resulted in racism. This is where the spider sits and from whence
his convoluted web emanates. Going back to the Tangled Web
illustration we see that there are other harmful spin-offs from
evolution besides racism. For example, we see that the "survival
of the fittest" mentality leads to narcissism, which leads people
away from the Savior and towards the everlasting fire. There are
other unsettling interwoven sins. Some were reviewed earlier in
this chapter. Rather than rehash each web, let me just leave you
with one overarching goal: kill the spider.

This thought was inspired by a daily devotional reading with
the same title.[27] Here is how it reads:

Kill The Spider!*

Read: Matthew 5:27–30

If your right eye causes you to sin, pluck it out. (Matthew
5:29)

Bible In One Year: 2 Samuel 1–2; Luke 14:1–24

We sometimes have mixed feelings about our sins. We are
afraid of being hurt by them, and we want to be forgiven. But
we aren't sure we want to be rid of them right now.

A man told me he has a bad habit that is hindering his fellowship with God and hurting his Christian testimony. He says he

---

* Herb Vanderlugt, Our Daily Bread, Copyright 2002 by RBC
Ministries, Grand Rapids, MI. Reprinted by permission. All rights reserved.

prays that God will forgive him for his addiction—but he doesn't stop. He reminds me of the story about the man who often went forward at the end of church services to kneel and pray, "Lord, take the cobwebs out of my life." One Sunday morning his pastor, tired of hearing the same old prayer, knelt beside him and cried out, "Lord, kill the spider!"

Yes, sometimes it takes radical action to break a sinful habit. We need to do more than ask God for cleansing each time we succumb to temptation. We must take whatever steps are needed to get the cobwebs out of our life. We must confess our sin and determine to be done with it. Then we must feed our mind with God's Word and do all we can to stay away from the people and places that tempt us to sin. That's what Christ meant when He said, "If your right eye causes you to sin, pluck it out." (Matthew 5:29).

Kill the spider and you'll get rid of the cobwebs. —HVL

It's not enough to say to God,
"I'm sorry, I repent,"
And then go on from day to day
The way I always went. —Anon.

Chapter Four Endnotes

1. Olaudah Equiano, *The Interesting Narrative of the Life of Olaudah Equiano, or Gustavus Vassa the African* (1789) quoted on Washington State University website http://www.wsu.edu:8000/~dee/Equiano.html.

2. Ken Ham, Carl Weiland, and Don Batten, *One Blood: The Biblical Answer to Racism* (Green Forest, AR: Master Books, Inc., 1999) 126.

3. Ham, et. al., *One Blood*, 126–127.

4. P.V. Bradford and H. Blume, *Ota Benga; The Pygmy in the Zoo* (New York: St. Martin's Press, 1992) 304 quoted in Ham, *One Blood*, 127.

5. Jean-Pierre Hallet, *Pygmy Kitabu* (New York: Random House, 1973) 292, 358–359 quoted in Ham, et. al., *One Blood*, 136.

6. Shipman, Pat, *The Evolution of Racism: Human Differences and the Use and Abuse of Science* (New York: Simon and Schuster, 1994) 77–78, 93, 94.

7. Shipman, *The Evolution of Racism*, 101.

8. Shipman, *The Evolution of Racism*, 132.

9. Shipman, *The Evolution of Racism*, 102.

10. Shipman, *The Evolution of Racism*, 111.

11 Shipman, *The Evolution of Racism*, 108, 116–117.

12. Shipman, *The Evolution of Racism*, 201.

13. Shipman, *The Evolution of Racism*, 178–178.

14. Note: Some very positive medical advances have come from the Genome Project as well.

15. Shipman, *The Evolution of Racism*, 226–229, 232–235.

16. Shipman, *The Evolution of Racism*, 236–239.

17. Ham, et. al., *One Blood*, 52–53.

18. Ham, et. al., *One Blood*, 58–59.

19. Ham, et. al., *One Blood*, 59.

20. Ham, et. al., *One Blood*, 59–60.

21. Ham, et. al., *One Blood*, 67.

22. Rebecca L. Cann, Mark Stoneking, and Allen C. Wilson, "Mitochondrial DNA and Human Evolution," *Nature*, 325 (London: Nature Publishing Group, 1987) 33.

23. Lee Strobel, *The Case for Faith: A Journalist Investigates the Toughest Objections to Christianity*, (Grand Rapids, MI: Zondervan-PublishingHouse, 2000) 96–97.

24. Dr. Walter Bradley quoted in Strobel, *The Case for Faith*, 101.

25. Dr. Walter Bradley quoted in Strobel, *The Case for Faith*, 101.

26. Ham, et. al., *One Blood*, 25.

27 . Herb Vanderlugt, "Kill the Spider," Our Daily Bread, (Grand Rapids, MI: RBC Ministries) April 17, 2002.

Chapter Five

The Devil is a Clever Liar

Ye are of your father the devil, and the lusts of your father ye will do. He was a murderer from the beginning, and abode not in the truth, because there is no truth in him. When he speaketh a lie, he speaketh of his own: for he is a liar, and the father of it. (John 8:44)

Who is the initiator and the instigator of this issue? It is the father of all lies, Satan himself. In the above passage of scripture, Jesus calls him out as such. He is a very practiced and clever deceiver and has used racism to distract people from salvation in Christ. In this chapter we will look at how this lie has affected people who are outside of the body of Christ. People who have not accepted Jesus Christ are outside of His body, outside of His protection. They are completely exposed to wiles of the devil because they do not recognize who he is or acknowledge what he is doing to them. If this is you, I must urge you again to repent and believe on Christ before it is too late.

Make no mistake about it Satan inspired racism through pride, greed, fear, and self-righteousness. Also understand clearly that he is an equal opportunity trickster. People, both white and black, have been deceived and used as his pawns. To reiterate, the world is not divided into black and white, nor haves and have-nots, but rather believers and unbelievers, the lost and the saved (Romans 8:9).

Let us examine how have blacks been deceived.[1] There is a widespread distrust of white people in the black community and it is based partly on the lie that all white people are overt racists. They are all focused on one main goal: keeping the black race down. They are all actively involved in this mission, some secretly and some openly. Many blacks think all whites support baton wielding, trigger-happy police and are all either Klu Klux Klan members or supporters. Some think these things in the deep recesses of their subconscious. Others are cognizant and express it openly. It is thought that white people are greedy gluttons who horde all of the best resources in this country and even the world for themselves—leaving people of color starving and in despair. White people one day discovered Africa and decided instantly that black people were inferior and should be their slaves. Then they went in with guns and held the continent hostage while kidnapping and plundering its innocent unsuspecting people.

We have already reviewed the complexity of the slave trade in chapter three and that dispels the latter myth. Concerning the former, I do not believe that white people are as racially obsessed as black people tend to be. There may be some radical hate factions that actively pursue these goals, but most white people live in ignorance of or simply disregard the history of this nation and its ramifications. It is only when confronted with an explosive racial issue or the outlook of a personal black friend or acquaintance do they begin to give cursory thought to the problem. On the other hand, many black people are keenly aware of racial overtones and incidents. It is an everyday part of life. I understand better this difference of perspective as a black person when I remind myself of my attitude as an American. I was vaguely aware that people in the Arab world felt oppressed by my country's privileges and its foreign policies. However, I certainly did not focus on it night and day, neither to further nor to combat the oppression. I had never even investigated enough to know if it was true. Not until September 11th, 2001, when Arab terrorists attacked the World Trade Center in New York, did I even see it as something that affects my life personally. I believe this is analogous to how the majority of white people see racism in this country. When confronted with it directly, they may acknowledge it as an issue, but otherwise they live in blissful ignorance as life's other pressing issues take precedence.

A second and related deception is that white people are the devil. Today we have black people who earnestly think that whites are the devil. This idea was very prevalent among black American Muslims during the Malcolm X era. The mistaken logic then flows that if white people are the devil's spawn, black people must be the opposite, the righteous ones. We have suffered so much pain by their hands that our suffering has become our salvation. Many blacks have been tricked into believing that our own heartache, strife and pain atones for our sins. We wallow in self-pity crying out Lord, Lord, look how much we have endured!

Before I received Christ as my Savior I, too, believed this. We black people, and myself in particular, deserved to go to heaven and get some peace and rest after all the racist hell we have caught here on earth. Satan is a great deceiver. The truth is that Christ suffered more than anybody and everybody who ever lived—combined. He took on the sins of the whole entire world and did all of the work of atonement on the cross. It is only when we put our trust in Him that we are redeemed. Only when we confess our sin and acknowledge that He has already paid for them can we be made whole. There is no greater suffering than to be separated eternally from God, which is the definition of damnation. No earthly suffering can match eternal damnation.

I was also one who relished my cultural history in a religious way. I read books on black history, the black struggle, black fiction, black people's trials and triumphs. I felt superior knowing that I had gotten to something the "white man" tried to deny. Sometimes it was so consuming as to be my only pursuit of pleasure outside of work. While my white co-workers had passions for baseball or crocheting for example, I was enthralled with my own self-righteous anger that grew according to all the knowledge I gained. However, our black heritage is not our salvation, either. Many blacks, like me, have turned this way for comfort and solace worshipping the false gods called "our heritage," "our unity," and "our suffering." Unity in the black community might be a good thing, but again, it will not save us. It may help us with earthly gains and creature comforts, however, we will not go into eternity unified. Instead we will have to be separated at death, the dark-skinned sheep from the dark-skinned goats.

> But we are all as an unclean thing, and all our righteousness are as filthy rags; and we all do fade as a leaf; and our iniquities, like the wind, have taken us away. (Isaiah 64:6)

The bottom line is that nothing we can do in our own strength can save us. Only Christ's blood can atone for our sins. No amount of suffering, good works, or knowledge can substitute for the real thing. While it is true that white people committed great atrocities during slavery and beyond, that does not make them the devil himself. He is the father of lies. Therefore he is the father of those whites who are not redeemed, but also of any unrepentant person of any race or culture. We have all sinned and fallen short of the glory of God. (Romans 3:23) Therefore, whoever says he or she has not sinned is a liar and the truth is not in them. (I John 1:8) They are easily manipulated by the master liar.

Here is yet another myth. Many black people, filled with the bitterness of the harsh hand racial oppression has dealt, believe that focusing on heaven is a con game. White people, along with black co-conspirators in oppression, are using Christianity to stop black people from exposing racism and demanding reparations and justice here on earth. Bob Marley sang in one of his popular recordings, "We're sick and tired of your . . . games, dyin' and goin' to heaven in Jesus' name." White people have somehow set our gullible minds on heavenly reward as some sort of pacifier to shut up our cries of injustice, or so it is thought. Ironically, the real truth is the total opposite. The devil is running a con game to try and stop people from ever considering their eternal destiny. If he can keep you focused on your immediate needs, the right here and right now, then you will be apt not to consider that eternity is infinitely longer than this life. This life does fade as a leaf and wither as the grass. Jesus said this:

> Lay not up for yourselves treasures upon earth, where moth and rust doth corrupt, and where thieves break through and steal: But lay up for yourselves treasures in heaven, where neither moth nor rust doth corrupt, and where thieves do not break through nor steal: For where your treasure is, there will your heart be also. (Matthew 6:19–21)

He also had this warning about earthly gain:

> For what shall it profit a man, if he shall gain the whole world, and lose his own soul? (Mark 8:36)

Imagine the most extreme case. What if black people in this country somehow became the most prosperous, most unified, most sought after community in this nation and the world? Black neighborhoods were the choicest places to live and black schools were the premier schools. What if also in the process the message of the gospel was abandoned and people gave all the credit to our ancestors, our strong heritage, our unity. Know this: it ultimately would be bad for those people. They might live happily on earth for 70, maybe even up to 100 years or more. However if they never saw the light of Christ, they would then spend eternity in torment just like the rich man in the Book of Luke (chapter 16, verses 19–31).

Another related lie in the cauldron of racism is that Jesus is the white man's God. Some black people believe that Jesus—our beautiful, kind, loving, humble, all-mighty savior,—is a white supremacist! They call Christianity the "white man's religion." They probably have been influenced by white supremacist groups, many of which claim to be Christians. Jesus is not a racist. He is not even a conservative Republican. He is the greatest radical who ever lived. He transcends all space, time, culture and politics. Even a cursory reading of any of the Gospels would dispel this myth. Listen to His words:

The Spirit of the Lord is upon me, because he hath anointed
me to preach the gospel to the poor; he hath sent me to heal
the brokenhearted, to preach deliverance to the captives, and
recovering of sight to the blind, to set at liberty them that are
bruised. (Luke 4:18)

These are not the words of an elitist or an exclusionary racist! Here we find concern for the poor, the least, and the left out.
Not only is there concern, but a mission to heal those who are
brokenhearted in this life.

Many black people have also been misdirected by the devil
to focus on whether Jesus was black or white. There has been a
great deal of energy and effort put forth to prove that Jesus was
indeed black. Even within the body of Christ there are a substantial amount of black people fixated on this issue. Mainly, however, Satan tries to keep unbeliever's attention on the amount of
melanin that was in Christ's skin or the texture of his hair. These
things distract them from the importance of His shed blood.

I recall once during a family gathering that a movie about Jesus came on television. People were milling and talking so the
movie was more like background noise. I, however, was watching and was really moved by one particular scene of Jesus' tell-
ing of the story of the prodigal son. Then one of my relatives
glanced at the TV. Her face contorted into a scowl as she sneered
at the TV. and said something like, "that white man is not my
god!" I was jarred out of my concentration and hardly knew
what to say. This was someone who claimed to be a Christian.
After the angry outburst she and everyone else went back to socializing as if nothing unusual had happened, as if she had just
stated a plain truth that could not be disputed. No one seemed
surprised to hear these thoughts vocalized. They had heard it all
before. I was dismayed, but to my discredit, failed to say anything.

It is the blood of Christ that washes away sin, not the physical skin on Christ. Suppose, for example someone wanted to give
you a gift. And let's say that you hate the color orange. However, it so happens that the gift is wrapped in bright orange paper. They tell you that the gift is a diamond worth a hundred

million dollars. Would you refuse that diamond because the wrapping offends you? NO!—That would be ludicrous because the covering is so relatively insignificant to the gift! The same is true of Jesus Christ. God so loved the world that He gave His only begotten son. (John 3:16) Jesus is a gift to the world. To reject this most precious gift because of the skin it is in would be likewise ludicrous. Popular gospel artist Kirk Franklin, in the lyrics for the tune "The Blood Song," questions why we focus so much on the color of Christ's skin, when it is His blood that really matters.[2]

Let us turn the coin over and review some of the common lies whites have believed about blacks. How have whites been deceived by racism? I reemphasize that these are generalizations that may not apply to every person. The first is that black people are immoral. Many whites think blacks are all thieves, rapists, murderers, prostitutes, dope fiends, and sex fiends. Blacks are unintelligent beings with undisciplined children. Their children bring the merit of a school down. Black families as a whole bring down the quality and property values of a neighborhood. Black women are hyper- sexual beings. Black men are sexually insatiable, probably because of the women and this flaw they carry. Some think these things in the deep recesses of their sub-conscious minds. Others are cognizant and express it openly. These lies lull white people into a false sense of superiority, a false security.

That brings us to the second deception; namely, that the cream of the crop goes to heaven. Many whites have been tricked into believing that they are morally superior to everyone else in the world, especially black people and therefore are heaven bound. They have been deceived into thinking that God will take the cream of the crop according to the world's standards of who appears morally better, more successful, more beautiful, etc. They have failed to acknowledge that "ALL have sinned and come short of the glory of God." (Romans 3:23) (emphasis mine).

> But we are all as an unclean thing, and all our righteousness
> are as filthy rags; and we all do fade as a leaf; and our iniqui-
> ties, like the wind, have taken us away. (Isaiah 64:6)

In contrast with God's perfect and pure holiness our own
self-righteousness is considered filthy. Regardless of how other
humans see us, to God we are all the same: sinners in need of
salvation.

Many whites have been deceived into believing that good
moral conduct and the conservation of an era gone by will save
them. Conduct that is considered "good" according to human
standards and being a political conservative will not get you into
heaven. Salvation is not of works, lest any man should boast
(Ephesians 2:8–9). Works are good for reward in heaven after
one has made his or her covenant with the Lord, Jesus Christ and
that is only if those works are according to God's will. Ephesians
chapter 2, verse 10 says that we are saved unto good works. In
other words we are inspired to good works by God's saving
grace, in response to His setting our souls free by the blood of
His son Jesus. Even though the moral conduct of America's past
appears to be more in line with the word of God, it has the gap-
ing flaw of being a period of great injustice and inhumanity towards black people. This is why many blacks resist American
nostalgia and patriotism.

While it is true that there are many social problems in economically depressed black communities, they have nothing to do
with the color of the people's skin. People of all cultures have
done deviant, devilish things. We are all susceptible to Satan's
lewd suggestions and promptings. Africans were astonished at
the base behavior and immorality of whites during the slave
trade. Olaudah Equiano, a slave whose memoirs of the Middle
Passage survived, expressed how he had never in Africa seen the
type of cruelty and brutality that he witnessed and experienced
on the slave ships.

> The first object which saluted my eyes when I arrived on the
> coast was the sea, and a slave ship, . . . These filled me with
> astonishment, which was soon converted to terror, which I am

at a loss to describe, . . . I was now persuaded that I had got into a world of bad spirits, and that they were going to kill me. Their complexions too differing so much from ours, their long hair, . . . if ten thousand worlds had been my own, I would have freely parted with them all to have exchanged my condition with that of the meanest slave in my own country. . . . I asked them if we were not to be eaten by those white men with horrible looks, red faces, and long hair.[3]

Whites have been tremendously deceived by revisionist history. Not only whites, but many other people including some blacks are confused by this sham. They tend to believe that Africa was an uncivilized jungle before Europeans arrived and showed the Africans the backwardness of their ways. This distorted view says that Africans actually benefited from slavery because it gave them contact with the "more advanced" European culture. It helped Africans to understand how organized, higher, human society should work. This is a widely accepted view. This is a boldfaced lie. It is one facet of the sin of racism that persists. The devil has inspired this revised view of history and therefore it very difficult to disprove.

Let me refute by plainly state the truth here. Anyone still in disbelief can study the issue further on his/her own. There was highly ordered civilization in Africa, which produced mathematicians, scholars, world travelers, builders, and even Popes.[4] Egypt is part of Africa, but there were ancient African civilizations even outside of Egypt. Take for example the city of Timbuktu. The building technology of that city was far advanced for its era having houses made of masonry with structured roofs, doors and windows, lime whitewash, and even some special two-story structures.[5] They had advanced agricultural technology because they produced a variety of complex crops: rice, corn, red maize, beans, pumpkins, okra, tomatoes, cucumbers, cotton, cocoa-nuts, pine-apples, and yellow figs.[6] They manufactured cotton cloth and were herdsmen of horses, cows, sheep, goats, and asses.[7] The city of Segu, for another example, was described by 18th century European visitor, Mungo Park, as being surprisingly civilized and magnificent.[8] There was advanced manufacturing technology in Africa before the holocaust. The Buono peoples were known for their gold refineries.[9] Senegambia had iron and copper industries and goldsmiths more accomplished than Europeans.[10] Other African empires included Kush, Benin, Meroe, Djenne, Ghana, and Songhay.[11] This is by no means a comprehensive list because there are records of many, many more achievements.

If these aforementioned ploys were not enough to dupe a white person, next Satan tries to perpetrate excuses. There are two particularly prominent ones that say that the slave trade was somehow justified. The first argument says that because slavery was already a custom in Africa before the holocaust that therefore the Mid-Atlantic slave trade was acceptable. A few of the surviving records indicate that slavery in many African cultures was very different from American chattel slavery. A human slave was not considered less than human, property, or no more than a horse or other animal. Human dignity was maintained in African slavery. This is not some romantic notion invented by modern descendants of Africans to paint a rosy picture of their past and culture. There are detailed personal accounts of the difference in treatment.

Olaudah Equiano tells of his attempted escape from his African slave master before he was shipped to the Americas. He had accidentally killed a chicken and ran away in fear of punishment. He went back because he was starving and in despair that he could not find the way home. His masters were so glad that he was safe and that this young boy had not perished in the wilderness that they only reprimanded him. They did not even beat him.[12] Before he was kidnapped and enslaved himself, he and his family owned slaves themselves. Here's how he describes the way his family treated slaves. The contrast is quite stark when compared to slavery in the West Indies:

> Those prisoners which were not sold or redeemed were kept as slaves: but, how different was their condition from that of the slaves in the West-Indies! With us they do no more work that other members of the community, even their master. Their food, clothing, and lodging, were nearly the same as [ours],

except that they were not permitted to eat with those who were free born; . . . Some of these slaves have even slaves under them.[13]

Another example is the saga of Ali Esami, whose journey into slavery highlights the sharp contrast between the slave experience in Africa and in America. He was kidnapped by other Africans as a young boy and sold to a Yoruban. It was typical for slaves to be enslaved in various places in Africa before being sold to Europeans. The Yoruban master asked Ali if he was a king, because he seemed to comport himself regally. Ali told him how his father was a scholar and the man said, "'his father must have been a fine man; I will not treat him ill.'"[14]

In stark contrast to his experience with the Yoruban master Ali describes his experience with white slave masters:

The [whites] of the great vessel were wicked: when we had been shipped, they took away all the small pieces of cloth which were on our bodies, and threw them into the water, then they took chains, and fettered two together. We in the vessel, young and old, were seven hundred, whom the white men had bought. We were all fettered round our feet, and all the oldest died of thirst, for there was no water. Every morning they had to take many, and throw them into the water: so we entreated God by day and by night, and, after three months, when it pleased God to send breezes, we arose in the morning, and the doors were opened. When we had all come on deck, one slave was standing by us, and we beheld the sky in the midst of the water.[15]

The second fallacy used to justify the slave trade is that it introduced Christianity to Africa and thus benefited these pagan nations. It is hard to believe that people actually bought into this lie, but there is historical documentation. The Code Noir, slave codes issued by Louis XIV and governing conduct in French Caribbean, had clear religious overtones.[16] Another Frenchman named Gerard Mellier published a report entitled On the Commerce of Nantes and the Ways to Increase It, which proved to be very influential in increasing the French slave trade.[17] "Mellier's

first supplementary argument was that the slave traders were res-
cuing slaves from 'error and idolatry' by taking them to a place
where they could be baptized and instructed in the Catholic religion."[18]

Christianity, however, had already been introduced in Africa
before the slave trade. In fact, the early African church has quite
a rich history. Initially, it flourished rapidly and had many mar-
tyrs of the faith as they spread the gospel of Christ throughout
the continent. The African church battled over matters of doctrine, allegiance to the Roman church under Constantine, and
pagan influences and interjections into the faith. The early African Christian church stood firm in its orthodox teachings until
the Byzantine Empire was conquered by the Muslims and Islam
thereby gained dominance in Africa. Some of the influential
leaders of the early Christian church hailed from Africa, namely,
Clement, Origen, Tertullian, and Athanasius.[19] Not only that, but
there had been three Popes of African descent in the early Christian church: Saint Victor I (189–99 A.D.), Saint Miltiades
(311–14 A.D.), and Saint Gelasius I (492–96 A.D.)[20] Imagine the
uproar in the Catholic Church today if a black Pope were to be
appointed. This indicates how deep the deception of racism runs.

All of these arguments against the revisionist history that has
many white people deceived are presented here in a very cursory
form. For anyone interested in furthering their understanding of
these things, I recommend these books to start:[21]

Roots—by Alex Haley
The Diligent—by Robert Harms
Cane River—by Lalita Tademy
Middle Passage—by Charles R. Johnson
Before the Mayflower—by Lerone Bennet, Jr.—reference book
Wake of the Wind—by J. California Cooper

In closing this chapter, let us be reminded that the battle
against racism is fraught with lie traps, subtle snares of deception, and innuendos ingrained on our collective cultural mind
that cause pain, confusion, and hurt. Contrastingly, our creator is
compassionate and deeply personal. He would that none of us

would suffer. He wants to break the bondage that these misconceptions have on both black and white people. If this is you, do not let the lies and the liar hinder you any longer from coming to know God through His son, Jesus.

Chapter Five Endnotes

1. In this chapter I am using broad generalizations to emphasize a point. Of course not every black or white person has the thoughts or attitudes described, but these are prevalent notions, myths, or widely held beliefs.

2. Kirk Franklin, *The Rebirth of Kirk Franklin*, "The Blood Song," (Englewood, CA: Gospocentric, 2002).

3. Olaudah Equiano, *The Interesting Narrative of the Life of Olaudah Equiano, or Gustavus Vassa the African* (1789) quoted on Washington State University website http://www.wsu.edu:8000/~dee/Equiano.html.

4. Robinson, *The Debt*, 18.

5. Curtin, *Africa Remembered*, 149, 180.

6. Curtin, *Africa Remembered*, 150.

7. Curtin, *Africa Remembered*, 150.

8. Curtin, *Africa Remembered*, 148.

9. Curtin, *Africa Remembered*, 159.

10. Thomas, *The Slave Trade*, 63.

11. Robinson, *The Debt,* 15.

12. Curtin, *Africa Remembered*, 84–88.

13. Curtin, *Africa Remembered*, 78.

14. Curtin, *Africa Remembered*, 212.

15. Curtin, *Africa Remembered*, 211–213.

16. Harms, *The Diligent*, 26.

17. Harms, *The Diligent*, 15.

18. Harms, *The Diligent*, 19.

19. Robert Appleton Company, The Catholic Encyclopedia, Vol. 1, "Early African Church," (1907) quoted on The Catholic Encyclopedia, online edition, (K. Knight, 2005), http://www.newadvent.org/cather/01191a.htm.

20. Robinson, *The Debt*, 18.

21. Note: These are secular writings and are not Christian or evangelical in nature.

Chapter Six

Is Christ Divided?

Now I beseech you, brethren, by the name of our Lord Jesus Christ, that ye all speak the same thing, and that there be no divisions among you; but that ye be perfectly joined together in the same mind and in the same judgment. Is Christ divided? (1 Corinthians 1:10,13)

In this passage of scripture the Apostle Paul pleads with the church at Corinth to be unified. Then he asks a very pointed question. *Is Christ divided?* It is a rather ridiculous question because there is only one answer. Those who were saved, who had accepted Jesus Christ as Lord and Savior of their lives made up *the* body of Christ at that time. Therefore they were one—*by definition.* They were one body. In the same way we, Christians that is, are one today. The question was largely rhetorical because no one would chop his or her own body in half. The question provokes thought and cuts right to the heart of the matter of racism today. And so I must pose the same question Paul asked of the Corinthians to the church of America. *Is Christ divided?* Is He like a clown with a line down the middle of his face and with one side painted white and the other black?

Later in his first letter to the Corinthians, Paul expounds on this analogy between the body of Christ and our physical bodies.

He demonstrates that the body is in fact one. Ideally all of the members operate in concert for the common goal.

> For as the body is one, and hath many members, and all the members of that one body, being many, are one body: so also is Christ. For by one Spirit are we all baptized into one body, whether we be Jews or Gentiles, whether we be bond or free; and have been all made to drink into one Spirit. For the body is not one member, but many. If the foot shall say, Because I am not the hand, I am not of the body; is it therefore not of the body? And if the ear shall say, Because I am not the eye, I am not of the body; is it therefore not of the body? If the whole body were an eye, where were the hearing? If the whole were hearing, where were the smelling? But now hath God set the members every one of them in the body, as it hath pleased him. And if they were all one member, where were the body? But now are they many members, yet but one body. And the eye cannot say unto the hand, I have no need of thee: nor again the head to the feet, I have no need of you. Nay, much more those members of the body, which seem to be more feeble, are necessary: And those members of the body, which we think to be less honourable, upon these we bestow more abundant honour; and our uncomely parts have more abundant comeliness. For our comely parts have no need: but God hath tempered the body together, having given more abundant honour to that part which lacked. That there should be no schism in the body; but that the members should have the same care one for another. And whether one member suffer, all the members suffer with it; or one member be honoured, all the members rejoice with it. Now ye are the body of Christ, and members in particular. (1 Corinthians 12:12–27)

Imagine what a tremendous witness for Christ it would be to overcome racism within the body of Christ. It would show that God is above all of our problems. He is capable of curing any earthly ill that we suffer. Nothing is too difficult for God. It would also demonstrate that there is something different about believers in Christ Jesus, a higher calling so to speak. The world would see that there is something on the inside of us that causes us to behave this way, to strive to be like Christ.

So why have we not done it yet? Stubbornness, ignorance, and apathy on our part are to blame. In our own flesh we do not want to deal with this issue. We also let the weight of the world discourage us. The world is having great difficulty grappling with racism. We have been influenced by the world's outlook on the issue that is either a sweep-it-under-the-rug mentality or a no hope mentality. We are looking at the earthly circumstances surrounding racism and letting that diminish our trust in the mightiness of the mighty God that we serve. However, there is a third force working here besides the world and our flesh, and that is our adversary. Satan has a vested interest in the continuation and proliferation of racism. In the last chapter we saw how he attempts to blind unbelievers with it, but he has this weapon trained on believers as well.

> And the Lord said, Simon, Simon, behold, Satan hath desired to have you, that he may sift you as wheat: But I have prayed for thee, that thy faith fail not: and when thou art converted, strengthen thy brethren. (Luke 22:31–32)

Yes, Satan desires to sift us, the true believers, like wheat. To fully explain this passage of scripture it is helpful to understand the agricultural analogy to which Jesus is referring. When wheat grows, it is covered in chaff, which is a lightweight crust on the grains. To sift the wheat the farmer would toss it into the air. The heavier grain would fall directly to the ground while the chaff blew aside with the wind. Therefore, the wheat is the good part that comes down during the threshing process. To extend this analogy to humans we could say that the saved people are the wheat, those who are not saved (yet) are the chaff. I believe that concerning racism, Satan already has the chaff deceived. They follow every which way the wind blows concerning the race issue. Satan in this particular passage went after Peter (called Simon in this passage), who played a major role in the establishment of Christ's early church. We think of Peter as wheat. He is also going for the gold, God's people, with racial deception. His mission: to kill, steal, and destroy.

[Satan] cometh not, but for to steal, and to kill, and to destroy.
(John 10:10a)

As part of his smear campaign against God, the devil coaxed
many purported Christians (by purported I mean self-proclaimed
or carnal at best) into involvement with the slave trade. There is
overwhelming evidence that these people defied the God living
within them [supposedly] to lust after profit and prestige. In order to effectively combat this issue, Christianity should face this
stain on our history forthrightly. It is key to understanding why
the body of Christ operates in a divided manner today. If we
openly confess that Christians were a major part of this sin called
the slave trade, then God will be faithful and just to forgive us
and to cleanse us of this particular unrighteousness. If we deny
or ignore this fact it will continue to be a hindrance in moving
forward and growing in grace. Let us be encouraged by our Lord
Jesus Christ because, as we see in that passage in Luke quoted
above, He prayed for us that our faith would not fail when we
come under these kinds of attacks from the enemy.

Slavery and Christianity are linked together in many people's minds. In the best-case scenario, there was silence on the
part of Christians of that time concerning the slave trade, because we do not see a great outcry from the church. A worse and
more likely scenario is that there was cooperation with the ones
orchestrating this dastardly deed. At the very worst, there is in-
stigation and participation by the church. There are surviving
records of the slave ships and slave fortresses. Names like "Gift
of God," "John the Baptist," and "Jesus" indicate the worst, an
entrenched involvement by the church in the slave trade.[1] It is
interesting how certain Spanish judges contrasted Indian slavery
to European. "The first judges in the Audencia of New Spain in
1530 pointed this out in a letter to Charles V when they wrote
that servitude in ancient America was very different from what it
was in Europe: for 'they treat slaves as relations, while the
Christians [emphasis mine] treat them as dogs.'"[2] Notice how
they categorize the slave-owners in a blanket statement as
"Christians." A very prominent Christian, King Ferdinand, was
involved in bolstering the slave trade. In 1510 this king, who was

dubbed the "Athlete for Christ" by the Pope, authorized the first large scale importations of slaves to the Americas.[3] Herein we find Christianity firmly linked historically to slavery.

Of course, only God can look into the human heart to know for certain whether or not a person is saved. Therefore, we humans cannot judge whether the people involved in the trade were true Christians or not. There are many who profess to be Christians, but have not truly accepted Christ as Lord and Savior of their lives. Jesus warned that this would happen (see Matthew 7:22–24). So we can say that because their actions do not line up with Christ's teachings that perhaps they were not truly His people anyway. Another argument could be that for some their actions were not deliberately malicious. Perhaps they did not see or understand the far-reaching evil effects of their proclamations and deeds. However, for the real Christians who were direct witnesses to the horrors of the Middle Passage, the irony and the error of connecting this heinousness to the name of the Lord must have been inescapable, leaving them without excuse if they said and did nothing.

As mentioned in the previous chapter, people had also succumbed to the deception that slavery helped to bring Africans to Christ. Historian Gomes Eannes de Zurara chronicled the start and escalation of slaving expeditions from Portugal. His descriptions indicate that these pioneer slavers thought themselves on a great missionary adventure to win souls for Christ.[4] Zurara, in his description of the first slaves landing in Portugal in 1444, wrote of the great agony of the African captives and the heart-wrenching scene as families and friends were split up and sold separately. He also describes Prince Henry, the ruler, as unmoved. He collected his tax on the import, forty-six slaves, and proceeded to give thanks that he was "saving so many new souls for God."[5]

Pope Nicholas V supported Prince Henry and the Portuguese slaving efforts with a formal edict. On January 8, 1454, from the Cathedral of Lisbon, he issued the bull Romanus Pontifex approving the Portuguese monopoly on slaving expeditions and raising hopes that the African people would be converted to Christianity. Preceding this edict was the bull Dum Diversas in

1452 that said unbelievers could be reduced to perpetual slavery. This was a reaction to the growing Islamic influence in West Africa.[6] However, Jesus never taught, "If they reject me, brutalize and enslave them." He said, "Follow me and I will make you fishers of men," (Matthew 4:19), meaning He would use His followers to bring other followers into the kingdom of God. Therefore, if these powerful historical figures had truly been listening and walking closely with the Lord, they would have tried to witness instead of make war.

There was a prominent Spanish lawyer, Bartolomé Frias de Albornoz, who publicized a scathing criticism of the Christian leaders for promoting chattel slavery. In his *Arte de los Contratos* published in Valencia in 1573, he indicated that "no African could benefit from living as a slave in the Americas, and that Christianity could not justify the violence of the trade and the act of kidnapping. Obviously, he thought, clergy were too lazy to go to Africa and act as real missionaries."[7] Unfortunately, Christian leadership responded to this opportunity for correction with more defiance against God. Fray Francisco de la Cruz, a Dominican friar, rebutted by saying that an angel told him that "'the blacks are justly captives by reason of the sins of their forefathers, and that because of that sin God gave them that color.' [That blacks] were descended from the tribe of Aser—he must have meant Isacchar— and they were so warlike and indomitable that they would upset everyone if they were allowed to live free."[8]

What is sad and amazing is that this flimsy lie overshadowed the truth of Albornoz's criticism. Men's hearts were overcome with greed and they wanted to press forward with the trade. Any excuse, even one as flimsy as a dream, would do. When Jesus issued the great commission (Matthew 28:19–20) for his followers to make disciples, this is not what He intended. These people were clearly misguided. Jesus did not say, go and conquer lands, dominate and enslave the people that they might be saved. He told us to preach, teach, and baptize. God's namesake is defiled when we add our own agenda and avarices to this basic command. That is what happened with slavery.

Olaudah Equiano, the enslaved African whose memoirs of the Middle Passage survived, gives us the African perspective as he eloquently points out the hypocrisy of these so-called slavery missions. Equiano also suspects those involved in this brutality to be only "nominal" Christians—meaning in name only.

> O ye nominal Christians! Might not an African ask you, learned you this from your God? Who says unto you, do unto all men as you would men should do unto you. Is it not enough that we are torn from our country and friends to toil for your luxury and lust of gain? Must every tender feeling be likewise sacrificed to your avarice? Are the dearest friends and relations, now rendered more dear by their separation from their kindred, still to be parted from each other, and thus preventing from cheering the gloom of slavery with the small comfort of being together, and mingling their sufferings and sorrows? Why are parents to love their children, brothers their sisters, or husbands their wives? Surely this is a new refinement in cruelty, which, while it has no advantage to atone for it, thus aggravates distress, and adds fresh horrors even to the wretchedness of slavery.[9]

Another sin of slavery committed by so-called Christians is eisegesis of God's holy scriptures. Eisegesis is the incorrect interpretation of the Bible, using it in a manipulative way to support a wrong deed or philosophy. In this effort to be forthcoming on Christendom's part in slavery let us clear the air by looking at the texts that were more frequently used to support racial oppression.

> Servants, be obedient to them that are your masters according to the flesh, with fear and trembling, in singleness of your heart, as unto Christ; (Ephesians 6:5)

This scripture was taken out of context, both literally and socially to make slaves believe God was for American slavery. It was used in isolation of its literary context. Ephesians chapter five and the beginning of chapter six speak about reciprocal relationships in the body of Christ. It explains how husbands should relate to wives and wives to husbands; how children should relate to parents and vice versa. Therefore, when it talks about how servants should obey masters it speaks also of the proper behavior of masters towards slaves.

> And, ye masters, do the same things unto them [meaning slaves], forbearing threatening: knowing that your Master also is in heaven; neither is there respect of persons with him. (Ephesians 6:9)

Masters were commanded to behave the same way toward their servants as their servants did to them. They were to be obedient to their slaves—as unto Christ! They were not even to threaten them, never mind to whip, rape, and torture them. They were to keep in mind that there is really only one master, and that He is the Master of all.

The social context of this scripture also reveals its true interpretation and intention. When the Apostle Paul wrote this letter to the church at Ephesus, slaves were common in the Roman Empire. However, it was not the de-humanizing chattel slavery of the Americas and was not meant to make slaves endure ungodly tortures. Christianity was on the rise in this empire and so Paul wanted to make clear that Christians understood they were all equal, being all servants of the most-high God. In fact in Ephesians 5:21 he wrote that Christians should "submit" to one another. The word "submit" meant to treat the other person respectfully (a different nuance than its meaning today). The overarching theme of these passages on relationships is to develop kindness, Godliness, dignity, compassion, and all kinds of good qualities in dealing with one another as Christians. The real intent is completely opposite of how it was misused.

Similar scriptures, such as Titus 2:9–10 and Romans 6:16, were misused in the same way. The same corrective reading is necessary. I know of older African American Christians who will not even read the Apostle Paul's letters because they feel he was responsible for keeping black people oppressed. They miss out on about two-thirds of the New Testament because of this! The Apostle Paul had no knowledge of the future evils that men would do, twisting God's word around for their own power. Paul died in the second half of the first century. Looking again at the timeline from the previous chapter we see that his letters would have been written in the time *before* racism began. Therefore, he could not have been a racist, or had ill will towards black people as a hidden agenda in his writings. Besides, if you truly understand God's Word, you know that all scripture is written under the inspiration of the Holy Spirit. God supervises everything that is written, therefore we can trust the Bible. Paul's letters, then, cannot be attributed to Paul alone.

Despite all these negative things, there is very good news. The gospel of Jesus Christ is so powerful and pure, that it was able to reach African people and enslaved African Americans not *because of* the slave trade, but *in spite of* it. For example Joseph Wright, another of the few Africans whose writings of their slave ship experience have survived, gives testimony of how he came to accept Christ in 1834 after his experience with captivity. He was kidnapped and headed for the Americas as a slave when his ship was recaptured by slavery opponents and re-routed to Sierra Leone. He was there taught to read in English and thereby was taught about Jesus.[10]

Samuel Crowther is another example. Crowther was a renowned African bishop in the late 18th century and is considered one of the great founding influences on modern Nigeria. He was also rescued from a slave ship by British antislavery patrols. After becoming ordained in the Anglican Church, he founded the Niger Mission. Initially this mission was African led and staffed, but by the 1880's the British traders and missionaries turned hostile toward Crowther and demanded control. Nevertheless, his testimony is still quite inspiring:

> [A]bout six months after my arrival in Sierra Leone, I was able to read the New Testament with some degree of freedom. . . . The Lord was pleased to open my heart to hearken to those things which were spoken by His servants; and being convinced that I was a sinner, and desired to obtain pardon through Jesus Christ, I was baptized on the 11th of December, 1825. . . . May I ever have a fresh desire to be engaged in the service of Christ, for it is perfect freedom![11]

On another bright note, even though there was no unified opposition to slavery by the Christian church, there are some examples of individuals who struck out against it. The earliest instance is Pope Pius II, who set a somewhat dubious example in 1462 when he condemned taking new West Africans converts to Christianity into slavery. He never, however, condemned the practice outright or showed any concern for the cruelty done to those who had not yet accepted Christ.[12] Another voice of opposition came from a Dominican Friar named Thomas de Mercado. He had observed the evil done on slave ships first hand and emphasized the sinfulness thereof. In his *Suma de tratos y contratos*, published in Salamanca in 1569, he decried the dishonorable practices used to get slaves from Africa. He also noted how the temptation of European goods for slaves inspired African greed. However, he also stopped short of condemning the practice as a whole.[13]

More ardent opposition came in the late 1500's from Frei Pedro Brandão, a Portuguese bishop of the Cape Verde Islands. He vehemently opposed the trade and argued for its end. Instead of enslavement he wanted blacks to be "baptized and then declared free."[14]

This is not a comprehensive list of those who spoke out. Various Catholic Popes and religious leaders were involved in the anti-slavery movement, a few during its heyday and a larger presence toward the end. "Pope Eugene IV condemned slavery in the Canary Islands in 1435 and ordered immediate manumissions (within 15 days). Other Popes condemning slavery included Gregory XIV (1591); Innocent XI (1686); Benedict XIV (1741), and Pius VII (1815)."[15] "Paul III explicitly attributed slavery to 'the enemy of the human race, Satan.'"[16] "In 1838 Gregory XVI condemned all forms of colonial slavery and the slave trade, calling it *inhumanum illud commercium.*"[17]

Fast forwarding to the abolition movement in America, we find one light shining so very brightly for Christ that his efforts bear special mention. His name was William Lloyd Garrison. He was not the only inspirational soul fueling the abolition movement, but he was considered the founder and catalyst. It is the way he did what he did that make his efforts so exemplary. His arguments against slavery were based on God's Word. He rightly divided the word of truth and applied it to the real life crisis at hand in order to affect positive change. He used the light that Christ placed in him to start a fire—the fire of change. That is why he is remembered as the father of the abolitionist movement in America.

These two quotes paint a vivid picture of him:

> The central fact of Garrison's life was his religious faith. The Bible was the only book he ever really read. He wrote in "the language of the Old Testament" and "had the zeal . . . of a Biblical prophet, combined with apostolic dedication."[18]
> Garrison "demanded that all who called themselves Christian act like Christ. He wanted to convert them. . . . He imitated Jesus in . . . affirmations of all-encompassing love."[19] He told freed slaves, "I espoused your cause because you were the children of a common Father, created in the same divine image, having the same inalienable rights."[20]

Garrison's view was that your position on slavery was an indication of whether you were a true believer in Christ or a fake Christian and a hypocrite. He argued, "how can you say you love God and hate your brother?"[21] His whole ministry was focused on exposing the anti-biblical practices of American slavery. He was zealous and passionate about this mission. Abraham Lincoln said of Garrison that he "set the freedom process in motion."[22] Southern states pointed to his repeated and scathing condemnation of their ways and his 'personal liberty laws' as the two reasons they seceded from the union.[23] Here is an example:

> Slaver fathers who refused to acknowledge, much less, provide for, their children "had denied the faith and were worse than infidels" (I Timothy 5:8). . . . Garrison deemed that ministers who claimed that there was nothing in the New Testament against slavery (ignoring, e.g., I Timothy 1:10 (slave trading a sin) and James 5:4 (defrauding workers of pay) were "a brotherhood of thieves," and "the deadliest enemies of mar-

riage, of the Bible, the weekly Sabbath, the Christian church . .
. and of revivals of religion."[24]
The religion of slave owners and traders was "a religion that
apologizes for concubinage, polygamy, heathenism—a religion that murders and steals." The Presbyterians and Congre-
gationalists "stole babies," Southern Baptists "sold girls for
wine for their communion tables." "[T]he American Church is
steeped in blood and pollution" so we must "turn from it with
loathing and abhorrence."[25]

He used all of the scriptures cited in this writing and many,
many more to expose the evils of slavery. He inspired Harriet
Beecher Stowe, the author of *Uncle Tom's Cabin* (1852) and
Frederick Douglas, who was the most prominent African American in the abolition movement. Many others were inspired by
him to repent of slavery and cease from practicing or supporting
the institution. Many enslaved blacks were motivated to seek
their freedom through the "writ of habeas corpus" because of
him.[26]

Fast forward again to today. How does all of this history affect us? After all, as Christians we are saved and have been forgiven of all our sins, right? Can Christians today be held ac-
countable for the sin of racism? Do we suffer from its
consequences? I would argue that even though we are saved, we
still suffer consequences from un-repented sin. That includes
racism and other ills that we do not confess. I adhere to the notion of generational curses: i.e. that the iniquities of the fathers
are visited upon the sons and daughters—unto the third and
fourth generation (Exodus 20:5). Unresolved issues get handed
down from generation to generation. It does not have to be this
way, because Jesus is the bondage breaker. He is able to break
the cycle of this curse, but only if we want Him to. Racism is an
individual as well as a corporate sin. Therefore, the body of
Christ today suffers of this inherited ailment.

Many would argue that these concepts of generational curses
and corporate punishment do not apply today because we are
under the new covenant, under grace. They would argue that the
American church today is not responsible for the iniquities of the

church of America of the past. Their argument would be that the church of Christ is worldwide and not nation-specific like the nation of Israel was under the old covenant. The Jewish people were a nation under God's direct theocratic rule. At that time the people, as a group, could repent and receive forgiveness and conversely also could be punished corporately.

For example, the generation of Israelites who were brought up out of Egypt were sentenced to wander in the wilderness for forty years because of their disbelief, murmurings, and complaining. They were not allowed to see the promise land. Another example is the wrath of God that came upon the Israelites of the northern kingdom when they broke away from worshipping the true and living God and decided to go after idols (Jeremiah 25). Their community decayed and they were eventually taken into captivity.

However, in the book of Revelation we see a new covenant equivalent because therein we see church groups being corporately judged. In chapters two and three of Revelation, Jesus goes through and judges the churches of the different states. He encourages and compliments the things they are doing right, but admonishes them strongly for their sins. To the church at Ephesus He warned that they have "left their first love" (Revelation 2:4), referring to Himself. The church at Pergamos was guilty of letting idol worshippers into their midst. Jesus warned, "Repent, or else I will come unto thee quickly, and will fight against them with the sword of my mouth." (Revelation 2:16) He told the Laodiceans that they made Him nauseas because they were "lukewarm." They were neither cold, completely dispassionate, or hot, passionate, about building God's kingdom. They were too middle-of-the-road.

What would Jesus say to the leaders of the churches of America? How would He judge the church of Europe concerning racism? Would He be sickened by our segregated worship? I see two large stumbling blocks to racial healing in the church of America: "The Social Gospel" and the "Right Wing Political Agenda." Is Jesus angered by our political and social agendas, our diversions from the pure gospel? The "black" church tends to overemphasize the Social Gospel, the "white" church the Right

Wing Political Agenda. Both these ills lead to what I call the double-minded church. These issues tend to take center stage, leaving the good news of salvation through Christ as an afterthought. I have heard numerous sermons dedicated mainly to the Social Gospel. At the end there is tacked on some mention of Jesus and Him crucified because it was time for the call to discipleship. I have also seen many people turned off by the white church because off its conservative political affiliation.

The Social Gospel is when black people use the Christian church to highlight racism in this country, to mobilize politically for the Democratic left, and to influence social policy like welfare and affirmative action. Some white people condemn this as a gross misuse of the church. There is nothing intrinsically wrong with the church dealing with social injustice. The problem comes when these things eclipse the mission of saving souls for Christ. This has actually happened in some black churches as collectives as well as to some individuals within black churches. But God has been our strength through the struggles against slavery and Jim Crow, racism and discrimination. He cares about social injustice and He does inspire many through these struggles. The problem is now that some are using the church *solely* for personal political gain or *solely* for promoting social change. That is not the great commission of the church. But unfortunately, everyone in the church today is not saved. This is the problem of the double-minded church. We cannot decide whether to focus on the worldly agenda or the heavenly agenda. The Bible is clear, however, that we should seek the kingdom of God *first* and all these other things will be added to us (Matthew 6:33)

Let us look more closely at the Right Wing Political Agenda. Many blacks accuse whites of using the Christian church to mobilize ultra-conservative right wing voters into political action that supports racist policies and Anti-Civil Rights legislation. And they do. That is some do, at least, because, unfortunately, everyone in the church today is not saved. This is the problem of the double-minded church. The kingdom of God is second behind pressing social and political agendas. If you asked many unbelievers what they think the mission of the mainstream

Christian church in America today is they would probably say to stop abortion, fight homosexuality, and keep the white race dominant. That is how I viewed the white church before I was saved.

Although these broad-brush accusations are only partly true, they damage our witness as a collective. In some instances the black church *has* been used to under gird Democratic candidates, without regard to those person's relationship to Christ. Whites *have* used the church to condemn black culture as inherently evil and morally inferior. Even as recently as the year 2000 a prominent Christian College, Bob Jones University, had a ban on interracial dating. "The school had justified its ban on interracial dating by saying that God created people differently for a reason."[27] This controversial issue came to the forefront of American politics when then presidential candidate George W. Bush gave a campaign speech at the college. The school has since dropped the ban, and explained away its origins as harmless. However the incident struck a nerve in the hearts of many black people that again lumped Christianity, racism, and right-wing conservative institutions together.

Liberals and conservatives have also had opposing perspectives concerning American history. The schism exists among Christians as well. From the conservative view, America was a good, moral, and pure country until the evil liberals gained power and affected change in the 1960's and 70's. They often imply that the changes of these decades demoralized the country. There is not very much care taken to distinguish the sexual immorality and increase in drug use/abuse from the Civil Rights movement. Those decades are simply demonized carte blanch.

Conversely, the liberal perspective paints America as an evil, slave-owning, Jim Crow, racist, segregated, hate-mongering place before the Civil Rights era of the 60's and 70's. Many black people hold this view. They see those same decades as the shining glimmer of redemption couched in a centuries long tradition of malice. I have heard liberal Christian commentators seriously call into question whether conservative Christians are true Christians at all. Ironically, I have also heard the exact opposite from conservative Christians. They question whether lib-

eral Christians are really saved. How then is the body of Christ
able to function properly while holding such opposing perspectives?

Because everyone in the Christian church is not saved we
have this problem of instability, of double agendas that work in
opposition. Jesus Christ is about love, compassion, forgiveness,
and salvation. Both the Social Gospel and the Right Wing Political Agenda, conservatives and liberals often are hateful, judg-
mental, and warring. It is not only those in the church who are
not saved, often even people who are saved are not focused on
the Lord Jesus Christ. The Social Gospel and the Right Wing
Agenda are their passion. The purpose of the body of Christ
called church is to tell a dying world about the good news of salvation through Jesus. We are called to be the light and the salt of
the earth. Jesus came not to condemn the world, but that the
world through Him might be saved (John 3:17).

Besides politics, music is another big part of the cultural divide. It has become our music verses theirs. We rationalize that it
is acceptable for the 11:00 hour on Sunday to be the most segregated hour in America because we have different cultural styles
of worship. It is more comfortable for us to worship with others
of similar background. We call black Christian music "Gospel"
and white Christian music "Christian." How did we get to this
bizarre state of separation? The songs are all praising the same
God. Sometimes even the same song is put forth in different
styles and one is called gospel music and the other Christian.
Two examples are "Our God is an Awesome God" and "Wonderful, Merciful, Saviour." Fortunately, God is still awesome
whether we praise Him with a rock music flavor or a southern
bluesy style. The Bible says to make a joyful noise. The different
cultural styles we have of doing that vary just as the members of
the body differ. This should be a point of enrichment as opposed
to division. It is a chance for cross-cultural exchange. Rick Warren in his book, *The Purpose-Driven Church*, makes the point
that there is no such thing as Christian music, only Christian
lyrics.

> I reject the idea that music styles can be judged as either "good" or "bad" music. Who decides this? The kind of music you like is determined by your background and culture. Certain tones and scales sound pleasant to Asian ears; other tones and scales sound pleasant to Middle Eastern ears. Africans enjoy different rhythms than South Americans.
>
> To insist that all "good" music was written in Europe two hundred years ago is cultural elitism. There certainly isn't any biblical basis for that view.
>
> What makes a song sacred is its *message*. . . . There is no such thing as "Christian music," only Christian lyrics. If I were to play a tune for you without any words, you wouldn't know if it was a Christian song or not.[28]

Some black Christians sell themselves short by limiting their musical praise repertoire to "Gospel" music. They never have heard the passionate guitar riffs of Steven Curtis Chapman, or the sweet voice of Nicole Nordeman. Whites who are restricted to only "Christian" music are missing out on the great psalmist lyrics of Fred Hammond and the down home gospel riffs of Mahalia Jackson as well as the contemporary Mary Mary.

If I had not expanded my repertoire I would have never heard many lyrics that provided inspiration for this writing. My musically eclecticism has led me to enjoy and be blessed by white "Christian" music as well as black "Gospel" music. One example is "Gather at the River" by Point of Grace. This song is about people reconciling with one another for Christ's sake and by His blood.[29] The lyrics for "Come Together" by Third Day, another popular "Christian" group echo these sentiments.[30]

While writing the earlier chapters recalling the pain of slavery and racism, I purposefully listened to the music of white Christian artists. They reminded me that some of my brothers and sister in Christ are white and with their music they have blessed my life. It is a growth process and I am still growing.

I have been very open to cross-cultural Christian experiences that are remote. I listen to diverse music as well as listen to teachers of various backgrounds on the radio. In fact, my favorite radio ministers are not from my culture. One is world-renowned Christian apologist Dr. Ravi Zaccharias who is Indian. Another is a messianic Jewish teacher named Reverend Lan Solomon. The third is the very well known teacher and writer, Dr. Charles Stanley. Dr. Hank Hannegraf, president of the Christian Research Institute and host the Bible Answer Man Radio talk show, has also influenced my walk heavily. When I initially heard his broadcast I was quite repulsed. Because of his manner of speech and his intonations I thought him an arrogant and condescending white man. He had some serious criticisms of popular black preachers that made me immediately defensive. So initially I would listen to him to try and find some flaw in his logic or his theology. However, after listening for a while, I found many of his arguments and advice very persuasive and Biblically sound. This radio ministry has turned out to be a tremendous blessing to me.

On a more direct level, however, I have been guilty of staying mainly within my culture for church membership and fellowship. My cross-cultural dabbling has caused me to notice things that disturb me within the black church, errors that we are prone to by operating in isolation from the mainstream church of America and the world. One is the idea that a separate, and what I call "remedial," type of teaching is necessary for black Christians to learn effectively. I actually heard a very prominent black preacher adamantly proclaim this from the pulpit. He discouraged the congregation from listening to another very influential Christian teacher, who was white. He said his teachings were too complicated and convoluted and we would not get anything out of them. The implication seemed to be that we needed a more base, a more rude type of teaching. According to him, black people really do not have the capacity to understand these popular white preachers and apologists. Most of the people assembled there that day actually clapped and cheered "Amen!" at his pronouncement. Sad indeed.

Prosperity Theology is another thing that seems to have disproportionately infected the black church. We are easy prey because we have such a high percentage of people living below the poverty level. The idea that God is going to give them things, those material acquisitions that are the signs of status and acceptance in America, is very enticing. This theology is a reaction to what I call Poverty Theology. This was when slave masters told slaves they should never focus on earthly gain, but should think of only of their reward in heaven. Thus they controlled them and manipulated them to accept their earthly suffering as God ordained. Both are wrong and extreme. God wants us to be content, as the apostle Paul said, whether "abounding or abased."[31] My question with regard to Prosperity Theology is this: why should God prosper us as black people? We are not being honest about why our communities are in such economic despair. Perhaps He will bring us out of poverty once we stand up and face the hard truths about our history and what should be done economically.

Another misguided school of thought is what I call the "Party-Hardy" theology. It goes like this: Black people, simply because of our physical inheritance, have the party-hardy gene. It is somehow in our blood. Therefore, we ought to feel free to go out and party hardy whenever and wherever we wish, despite the fact that our Christian witness may be compromised. The African spirit of celebration in our bones should be honored. We should not let our sterile white Christian forefathers force us into a joyless, unnatural state. Party and drink out in the clubs on Saturday if you wish, and then come to church the next morning and party there, too! No guilt, no shame and shame on those who would try to make you feel guilty.[32] While it is true that our African culture has influenced our style of worship to be very lively, I disagreed that we need to express that in the secular as well. We have to be careful to guard our Christian witness in all situations.

Many blacks that are mature in the word of God are afraid to speak out against popular, but misguided teachings such as these because of fear of being ostracized or labeled a traitor. If someone is black and popular, we of the same race cannot criticize or disagree, but we must support in the name of black unity. Here is a word of advice for those afraid to challenge unsound doctrine:

> Preach the word; be instant in season, out of season; reprove, rebuke, exhort with all long suffering and doctrine. For the time will come when they will not endure sound doctrine; but

after their own lusts shall they heap to themselves teachers,
having itching ears; And they shall turn away their ears from
the truth, and shall be turned unto fables. But watch thou in all
things, endure afflictions, do the work of an evangelist, make
full proof of thy ministry. (II Timothy 4:2–5)

Now, I would imagine that there are things that are problem-
atic in the white church also because of the lack of cross-cultural
influence. However, I do not know what they are having never
been a member. Perhaps they need more lively services. One
thing I did notice while attending a racially mixed church conference is that many of the white people seemed very inhibited
from crying openly or lifting up their hands in praise during the
very spirited parts of the worship led by black people. At one
conference a black woman testified about the intense suffering
and trials she went through while struggling with a very advanced case of a debilitating disease. Every black person I could
see was moved to tears about how she had to rely only on the
Lord and how He did eventually heal her. The white people
around me seemed extremely uncomfortable and tense. They
seemed to purposefully steel themselves against showing any
emotion.

I have noticed that worship in the black church tends to be
more emotional, livelier than in the mainstream. I often wonder
how many white Christians, if they did not feel trapped by their
culture, would actually prefer to worship in a more lively fash-
ion. On the other hand, there may be many black Christians who
feel coerced into spirited worship at their churches when they
would actually prefer a more quiet and calm praise. Perhaps they
would prefer a meatier message from the pulpit even though it
may not have the style and fire that is traditional in the African
American church. To be honest, at times there is a lot of style in
these types of messages but not a great deal of substance.

Dr. Tony Evans summed up the situation very eloquently in
a sermon he preached called *Christianity and Culture: The Issue
Isn't Black or White.* In it, he said these words:

Our cultural differences must always be subservient to the spiritual needs of others. . . . The Lord's bottom line—and ours—is this: When culture comes into conflict with what God has said in His Word, culture is wrong and must be rejected.

Racism has also affected my personal Christian walk. At times I have been guilty of allowing it to take priority over my Christianity. I am growing and learning each day to combat this problem, however, anger can still well up inside of me with certain promptings. For example, when someone makes a racist comment, or a historically revised statement I have to fight the bile of anger that rises within me and I struggle to maintain Christ-like thoughts and demeanor. When I experience discrimination personally, my gut reaction is to defend myself and fight against it instead of letting the Lord fight the battle for me. I know other black Christians have had similar experiences.

Another example is how I struggled for years within my profession against the division of labor that runs along the color line. I am an architect and in my line of work the designers are in control of the aesthetics of the project. I have often felt a concerted effort to dissuade and exclude me and other black people from this area of work. I have been encouraged to stay on the more technical end of the work, the area that does not require much client contact or client confidence in my creative abilities. This has been a source of much anguish and anxiety for me for many, many years. But I am learning to leave it up to the Lord.

Sometimes I have trouble witnessing to white people. I start thinking about their demeanor and begin judging them for being racist, or snobby, or spoiled. I once had a job opportunity where I had very young, white co-workers. I found a lot of their conversation distasteful and their likings hard to relate to, so I spent most of my time by myself. I withdrew from them when I should have tried to befriend them like Jesus would have. The apostle Paul advised that we should meet people where they are and try to work with them. Instead, I found them such a culture shock that I abandoned and judged them. They in turn snickered and ridiculed me, not only for my Christian beliefs, but also racially. It was a vicious cycle and eventually I left the company.

On the other hand, I consider myself blessed because my first major encounter with racism did not occur until I was in high school. Before that I had had racial slurs and insults hurled at me, but those did not really hinder me my achievement. However, when I was in the tenth grade, I wanted to be on the cheerleading squad. At that time, my school could have been the poster child for racial integration. We had the perfect blend of ethnicities. About half the school was black and Puerto Rican and the other half was white and Portuguese. Every spring, when it started warming up, we could expect race riots to break out at our school. It was like an annual event.

The cheerleading squad, however, did not reflect the mix of the student body. The year I tried out, there were no black girls on the squad and as far as I know there never had been. Three of us tried out that year. One girl had extensive gymnastic training and was able to do back flips and things that no one else on the squad or trying out could do. There was no way to deny her a spot. She made the squad and went on to eventually become one of the captains of the team. I was no gymnastic marvel, but I had been practicing my cartwheels, splits, and jumps for years in anticipation of this moment. The feedback that I got was that I had excellent skills and did very well during the tryout. The other black girl was tall and lanky, (not your typical cheerleader build) and of average skill. Then there was this one particular white girl who tried out. She was very, very popular, and from a well to do family. She was smart, and blonde-headed. However, she had very little athletic ability. Her splits were pitiful. As it turned out, she was selected for the squad, while me and the other black girl were rejected.

I was heartbroken by this. Clearly they had selected the white girl of mediocre skill over me because I was black. My parents and I complained to the faculty cheerleading coach, who did the selecting. I blamed him for being a racist. We went also to the principal. He denied my claim and my parents told me to just forget about it. Loving teachers who saw my pain comforted me by saying I did not really want to be involved with that group of girls anyway as many had very bad reputations. The other black girl's mother however, went up to the school and complained vehemently and persistently. She threatened protests and media attention. In that racially charged climate that was enough. They decided to add a second alternate position so her daughter could be on the squad. Once again I was floored. Why didn't my parents persist? Where was the justice here? Why didn't they add a third alternate position for me?

Well, some of you may be wondering how I can recall this incident with such great clarity and detail. I am, after all, now well into my adult years and this happened in my second year of high school. Every time I saw the cheerleaders at school with their pom-poms and every game that I went to, I was envious and bitter. I would fantasize about what it would be like to walk around the school with my pom-poms chatting excitedly with the other girls about practice that day. I wondered what would it be like to be out on the floor during basketball games leading the crowd on in cheers. You may be wondering why I did not just get over this incident as my parents had suggested. It was only cheerleading for goodness sake! Even though these seem like very superficial desires and this incident seems very light, it really made me bitter about racism. This was the milestone incident that set my young mind on racial justice.

From high school, I went on the study at the prestigious Massachusetts Institute of Technology and the University of California, Berkeley. I studied architecture. However, when I came out of graduate school, the economy was in a slump. There was very little hiring going on in my field and I struggled for months to get a job. Finally, a family acquaintance gave me a chance and hired me. He was a black man. I was determined only to work for black firms after that. But this was not the best thing for me and God saw that. He eventually introduced a mentor into my life, a white woman, who blessed my architectural development in a tremendous way. I eventually ended up working for two very prominent white firms because of her influence. The point I make here is that my racial stubbornness, my racial scars and pride would have prevented me from these opportunities had God not stepped in and changed my plans.

As I mentioned earlier, national issues like the Rodney King incident and the O.J. trial have also affected me personally. They have strained relationships with others and my witness for Jesus at times. I also must be truthful and admit that I at times get angry and annoyed with my white brothers and sisters in Christ who are conservative. I do not trust their judgment and their political actions because I believe their outlook is colored by racism.

Conversely, however, I think about white people who have blessed my life. For example, my very best friend when I was growing up was white. She and her family were such a blessing to my life. I carried a great deal of guilt and pain when, in high school, I severed our friendship because I wanted be unified with my race. I did not want to be seen as a "white girl" because of having a best friend who was white. Years later, after I was saved, I contacted her and apologized for the way I had behaved. I have also had some very special and caring teachers and mentors who were white. The professional mentor I mentioned also guided me through the very difficult architectural registration process. She just happens to be a blonde-haired, blue-eyed white woman. I deliberately remind myself of these things when I encounter racism and my anger threatens to swell.

I must again emphasize the potential we have in the Christian community to be the shining example to the rest of the world regarding racial healing.

> A new commandment I give unto you, That ye love one another; as I have loved you, that ye also love one another. By this shall all men know that ye are my disciples, if ye have love one to another. (John 13:34–35)

In fact we see in this scripture that loving one another is a mandate from Christ because it is said in command form. It is an example to the world as to what the power of love can do, but more importantly it is a witness for Jesus, that we can do all things through Him because he strengthens us. Because He loves us so much, we can love each other. Because He has saved us and made us new creations, we can walk in newness, the newness of life, concerning racism.

This mandate applies to all nationalities and ethnicities of Christians where cultural barriers are concerned. Because black people have suffered under "Christian" oppression, those of us whom Christ has called anyway have a key role to play. We need to witness to others around the world that may be hindered by this perception of Christianity. They may be missing out on their blessing of knowing Christ because blindness caused by racism. One of my favorite teachers, Ravi Zaccharias, touched on this subject in his excellent and inspiring sermon entitled "The Spurious Glitter of Pantheism." In it he talked about how Hinduism first gained a foothold in America by laying the blame for colonialism at Christianity's feet. Americans who wanted to disassociate themselves from the guilt and blame of plundering and pillaging the world were drawn away to this foreign god. He pointed out also that this is how the religion has kept its stronghold in the eastern world. Then he related how once after he had lectured on this subject, an Indian man stood up during the question and answer period and said that the only reason he listened to the arguments for Christ on that evening was because Dr. Zaccharias is Indian like him. He would not have heeded a white man. Black Christians have that same anointing and we need to be aware of our similar influence on black unbelievers.

Jesus himself prayed that we would be one. In the first verse of the following scripture, He prayed for the original disciples and then the believers throughout the ages, including those of us today who have trusted in Him alone for our salvation.

Neither pray I for these alone, but for them also which shall believe on me through their word; That they all may be one; as thou, Father, art in me, and I in thee, that they also may be one in us: that the world may believe that thou hast sent me. And the glory which thou gavest me I have given them; that they may be one, even as we are one: I in them, and thou in me, that they may be made perfect in one; and that the world may know that thou hast sent me, and hast loved them, as thou hast loved me. (John 17:20–23)

In verse 21 Jesus points out that our oneness is our witness. We should be one so *that the world may believe* that Jesus is

Lord, sent by the Father in heaven as the Lamb of God who takes
away the sins of the whole world!

Also, during His ministry here on earth, Jesus proved that he
is able to take adverse groups and put them together peaceably.
This, once again, demonstrates His power to change hearts and
minds despite cultural barriers. The passage below talks about
the early Christians, some of which were Jewish and some Gentile. The context of this scripture is that they were at odds concerning the Jewish law of circumcision. Some of the Jewish believers were contending that this rite still must be adhered to in
order for someone to be saved. Many of the Gentile believers
disagreed.

> But now in Christ Jesus ye who sometimes were far off are
> made nigh by the blood of Christ. For he is our peace, who
> hath made both one, and hath broken down the middle wall of
> partition between us; Having abolished in his flesh the enmity,
> even the law of commandments contained in ordinances; for to
> make in himself of twain one new man, so making peace; And
> that he might reconcile both unto God in one body by the
> cross, having slain the enmity thereby: (Ephesians 2:13–16)

In the first sentence we see that these two groups of believers
were distant, or "far off" from one another. Then the writer
makes the very powerful point that the distant groups are made
close by the power of the blood of Jesus Christ. We as black and
white believers are closer than we know, closer than our behavior would indicate. Christianity may very well be the largest
multi-cultural entity in the world. In the last part of this quote is
the proclamation that answers the question posed in this chapter:
Is Christ divided? In the fullness of Himself He is able to make
two disparate groups into one, "reconcil[ing] both unto God in
one body by the cross." Thus he makes peace. He is not a clown
with a split face. Through Christ who strengthens us, we as black
and white believers are able to overcome all obstacles to be one.
Through Himself, He makes even the black man and the white
man one!

There is *one* body, and *one* Spirit,

even as ye are called in *one* hope of your calling;
One Lord, *one* faith, *one* baptism,
One God and Father of all, who is above all, and through all,
and in you all.
(Ephesians 4:4–6)

Chapter Six Endnotes

1. Vincent Harding, *There is a River: The Struggle for Freedom in America* (New York: Harvest/HBT Book, reissue edition, 1993) quoted on The Mariners' Museum website, "Resistance and Endurance" Captive Passage: The Transatlantic Slave Trade and the making of the Americas, http://www.mariner.org/captivepassage/departure/dep015.html.

2. José Antonio Saco, *Historia de la Esclavitud Africana en el Nuevo Mundo*, 3 vols. (Paris, 1879) [6,14], I, 158, quoted in Hugh Thomas, *The Slave Trade: The Story of the Atlantic slave Trade: 1440-1870* (New York: Touchstone, 1997), 105.

3. Hugh Thomas, *The Slave Trade: The Story of the Atlantic slave Trade: 1440-1870* (New York: Touchstone, 1997), 13, 92-93.

4 Thomas, *Slave Trade*, 56.

5. Thomas, *Slave Trade*, 21-22.

6. Thomas, *Slave Trade*, 65.

7. Thomas, *Slave Trade*, 146.

8. Discussed in Marcel Bataillion, *Bulletin Hispanique* 54, 368 quoted in Thomas, *Slave Trade*, 147.

9. Equiano, *The Interesting Narrative,* quoted on http://www.wsu.edu:8000/~dee/Equiano.html.

10. Philip D. Curtin, *Africa Remembered: Narratives by West Africans from the Era of the Slave Trade* (Prospect Heights, Il.: Waveland Press, Inc., 1997), 332-333.

11. Curtin, *Africa Remembered,* 315.

12. Thomas, *Slave Trade*, 71-72.

13. Thomas, *Slave Trade*, 146.

14. Discussed in Marcel Bataillon, *Bulletin Hispanique*, 54, 368 quoted in Thomas, *Slave Trade*, 147.

15. The Crime Prevention Group, "Roman Catholic Church Opposition to Slavery," (Leroy J. Pletten, 1999) http://medicolegal.tripod.com/catholicsvslavery.htm.

16. Lane Core, Jr., "The Catholic Church and Slavery," website http://ic.net/~erasmus/RAZ168.HTM (Lane Core, Jr. 1997) quoted on The Crime Prevention Group, "Roman Catholic Church Opposition to Slavery," (Leroy J. Pletten, 1999) http://medicolegal.tripod.com/catholicsvslavery.htm.

17. The Crime Prevention Group, "Roman Catholic Church Opposition to Slavery," medicolegal.tripod.com.

18. Prof Russel B. Nye, *William Lloyd Garrison and the Humanitarian Reformers* (Boston: Little, Brown and Co, 1955), 199–200 quoted in The Crime Prevention Group "Abolitionists Opposing Slavery and Tobacco," (1998, 1999) http://medicolegal.tripod.com/abolitionists.htm#Garrison.

19. Truman Nelson, *Documents of Upheaval: Selections from William Lloyd Garrison's THE LIBERATOR, 1831–1865* (NY: Hill and Wang, 1966), xvii quoted in The Crime Prevention Group, "Abolitionists," medicolegal.tripod.com.

20. Nye, *Garrison and the Humanitarian Reformers, supra*, 199, quoted in The Crime Prevention Group, "Abolitionists," medicolegal.tripod.com.

21. 1 John 3:10–17.

22. The Crime Prevention Group, "Abolitionists," medicolegal.tripod.com.

23. The Crime Prevention Group, "Abolitionists," medicolegal.tripod.com.

24. The Crime Prevention Group, "Abolitionists," medicolegal.tripod.com.

25. Nye, *Garrison and the Humanitarian Reformers, supra*, 136–137, quoted in The Crime Prevention Group, "Abolitionists," medicolegal.tripod.com.

26. The Crime Prevention Group, "Abolitionists," medicolegal.tripod.com.

27. Evangelical Press, "Bob Jones University Drops Interracial Dating Ban" Christianity Today, March 6, 2000 http://www.christianitytoday.com/ct/2000/10/53.0.html.

28. Rick Warren, *The Purpose Driven Church: Growth without Compromising Your Message and Mission*, (Grand Rapids, Michigan: Zondervan Publishing House, 1995) 281.

29. Joel Linsey and Regie Hamm (writers),Tony McAnany, (producer), "Gather at the River," recorded by Point of Grace, Rarities and Remixes, compact disc, (Paragon Music Corp, 1994).

30. Mac Powell, Samuel Tai Anderson, Brad Avery, David Carr, and Mark D. Lee (writers), Monroe Jones (producer), "Come Together," recorded by Third Day, *Come Together,* compact disc, (New Spring Publishing, Inc/Vandura 2500 Songs, 2001).

31. Philippians 4:10–13.

32. Rev. Xolani Kacela, "Do Good Christians Party," (Dallasblack.com: Sept. 3, 2002)

http://dallasblack.com/cgi-bin/main.pl?state=show_article&id=61.

Chapter Seven

God's Way is the Best Way

We have seen man's attempts to solve the problem of racism. Some efforts were quite valiant and I especially appreciate the ones that were based on faith in God and grounded in His word. I mentioned William Lloyd Garrison and the abolitionist movement. We heard also from Frederick Douglas and other opponents of slavery. The history-making events of the Civil Rights movement, with Dr. Martin Luther King Jr. leading the charge also bear special mention as a tremendous milestone in the healing process. I admire and appreciate the courageous warriors who have fought for the gains gotten this far. We have fought each other (the Civil War) trying to purge ourselves of this dark stain. We have tried to legislate this sin away through the Civil Rights Movement. Many of us have tried to ignore this issue away. However, and I must put this very delicately, in spite of these great strides, there is still a piece of the puzzle missing. All of these efforts and yet residuals remain. Why? The root cause has not been attacked and ousted. It seems that the soul of the issue still seethes menacingly just below the surface of the American conscious in all that this nation does. That is how we know we are not fully healed and that we are still hiding some issues. There has not yet been a battle in this war on racism that focuses exclusively on the spiritual healing available through Jesus Christ. Because of this, the gains we have enjoyed on the legal, political, social, and economic front are not fully complete. Jesus Christ is the spiritual bondage breaker. He tears down unseen strongholds and breaks chains that bind the heart and soul. We have not yet been spiritually healed from the scars of slavery and racism. Therefore, I want to go more in depth into the spiritual warfare we are facing now and the cleansing process that must take place for full healing to occur.

I also give credit to the "Black Power" movement for allowing us, as African Americans, to vent our anger and express our deep sorrows to the masses. However, while anger can be a motivator of certain actions, it does drain the soul. After the novelty of the exhilaration wears off, the soul is left empty. It is not true spiritual healing. Besides being fueled by anger and hatred, this movement had many other problems. For example, it has led us into a protest/reaction-ism mindset. We react to racial injustices when they occur instead of being proactive about positive solutions to the ongoing issues facing our communities. Mass protests have lost a lot of their effectiveness because of the lack of novelty, support, and media coverage. Also, the issues are not as straightforward as in the 1960's. Who and why to boycott, picket, and protest has become muddled in many cases.

Another obstacle, or sign as it were—signaling us to go another way, is the denial/pluralism mindset. Many white people, along with a surprising number of blacks, feel that we have arrived. The problem was solved through integration and desegregation or so it is thought. We have racially mixed neighborhoods, schools, and workplaces. This is definitely true and is a positive thing. However, we still have many segregated neighborhoods, schools, and work "arenas." There remain places where black people are stuck, such as inner-city schools. There are also places where we still are not allowed to go, such as work assignments protected by glass ceilings. There are also black and white people living and working side by side who never get to know each other. That is what pluralism is. People are not living cohesively together, but are simply tolerating each other's proximity without benefiting and learning from the contact. All of these are man's ways, the results of human solutions.

Granted, some of the events in the history of this battle against racism can be seen as God working through man to establish justice here on earth. Yes, they had secular goals, but God inspired the battles and empowered the people for the victories. Take for example the slave revolts. The slaves finally got together to stand up and say, "no, this is wrong, inhumane, and ungodly." The Civil War where people were inspired to fight and even die to rectify the situation can be looked at in this light.[1] The Civil Rights movement sprung from the black church. I myself am a product and beneficiary of the affirmative action era. I thank God for all of these blessings. Because of these I know that He does care about suffering and sorrow. I believe He was directing certain people toward these paths to accomplish these goals. A specific example is Denmark Vessey. He was an enslaved Christian preacher who made history by leading a slave revolt. He, like William Lloyd Garrison, was spiritually convicted through studying the Bible that slavery in America was definitely anti-Biblical. He saw in the Old Testament how slaves were only supposed to be held for seven years according to God's law (Exodus 21). This and other readings made him understand why his oppressors did not want him to be able to read the Bible for himself. It explained why they wanted to lie about God's Word and make him and other black people believe that God was for American slavery. His study of the real Word of God inspired him to revolt against the unjust system of perpetual slavery in America.

What I am trying to distinguish here is that these movements, while monumental and just, did not have an overarching evangelistic goal. Man's ways, the human solutions to this issue, have helped many people on this side of Jordan. They may have even inspired people to seek God's face and become saved through the power of the atonement Jesus has provided. I certainly hope so. However, that would have been a residual effect, a sidebar, to the main agenda. My concern is that many may have been freed from slavery because of the Civil War, and many more gained freedom and satisfaction from the victories of the Civil Rights Movement. But oh how tragic it would be if they, after experiencing worldly victories here on earth, died without ever knowing the spiritual victory of being in Christ Jesus and therefore had to be separated from God for ever and ever! It does not profit anyone to gain the whole world and then lose his very soul (Matthew 16:25–27). There is no earthly gain that is worth forfeiting eternal life with Christ.

> Jesus saith unto him, I am the way, the truth, and the life: no man cometh unto the Father, but by me. (John 14:6)

God's way is the best way. His way is the way of truth. It is the life-giving way, and it is the *only* way. Two important truths to ponder here are these: number one: White people are not God, and number two: Black people are not God. To say that the way to eliminate racial strife if for black people to become more like whites, integrating with them, looking like them, talking, dressing, and thinking like them is incorrect. Some believe that if only black people would assimilate, like other groups who have come to this country, then there would not be such a fear and disdain of our ways and our culture. To say that the white way is the right way is wrong because white people are not God. Aspiring to their standards for approval, justification, happiness, will not make anyone whole. White people sin and fall short of the glory of God—just like everyone else on the planet.

Conversely, to believe that white people should have to bow down to black culture as some form of repentance is also ridiculous. We black folks sometimes want white people confess that they are wrong and we are right. We would like them to concede that our ways are better than theirs, our thoughts higher than their thoughts. We want them to reject their own culture and long to imitate ours for acceptance just as we have been forced to do for so long. If they would suffer through all these things then, perhaps we might finally forgive them and release them from their guilt. This is idolatry and misplaced worship. The mainstream American culture is getting weary of tiptoeing around the very fragile cultural sensitivities of black Americans, who only represent 12% of the population. Of course we want the issue of racism to be resolved and wrongs to be corrected. We, like the Jewish people, do not want this nation and the world to forget about our Holocaust. However, black people should not expect worship—because black people are not God. Only God is God and from His perspective, there is none righteous—no not one. (Romans 3:10)

How then can we be healed spiritually from the un-repented, corporate sin of racism? What we need is a corporate healing. Corporate healing and wholeness can come in a similar way as individual cleansing from sin. It will not mean salvation and eternity in heaven for everyone in the nation, but it will mean breaking the bonds for many, hopefully great multitudes. A note of clarification is in order here. I am not proposing we create a Christian state in America, whereby the government forces our beliefs on all of the citizens of this nation. That is what Islamic governments do. I cherish the right to religious freedom that we as Americans enjoy. We as Christians cannot force anyone to accept Jesus Christ. The Holy Spirit has to convict them of sin and they have to be drawn by the Father to the Son.

Spiritual freedom comes from knowing the truth. We have already established that Jesus Christ is the truth. He defeated sin and death on the cross and on the third day He rose up from the grave with *ALL* power in His hand (Mark 29:18). He has the power to heal us from even this deep-rooted dilemma. He has the power to free us spiritually.

And ye shall know the truth, and the truth shall make you free. (John 8:32)

If the Son therefore shall make you free, ye shall be free in-deed. (John 8:36)

God has given us the perfect solution. We remain in bondage to hatred, bitterness, anger, and fear by choice.

To take advantage of the freedom offered by Christ Jesus we must submit to the cleansing process of God. It is a three-pronged process involving 1) Confession, 2)Repentance, and 3)Forgiveness. Individuals receive the gift of God's gracious forgiveness through confession and repentance. On the corporate level, this nation must also confess admitting that we have sinned against God by making humans into chattel slaves and forcing them to endure gross torture and inhumanity. There was a maelstrom of controversy when former President Bill Clinton suggested the nation formally apologize for slavery. He was on the right track. Unfortunately he backed down from the challenge. We must face the fact that the consequences of this sin linger on. We must acknowledge that slavery is an unresolved issue, that it is in fact the cause of today's racial bondage. We must face the whole horror of these truths, ugly and uncomfortable as they may be. Confession implies contrition. We must apologize for this sin—to God first, and then to the descendants of slavery.

Repentance is the second step. The word literally means "to change direction." There must be a spiritual change in direction in the way our nation deals with this issue. I believe once we have the courage to admit the sin and see the consequences, there will be apology as well as restitution as a result. The poverty and despair in black neighborhoods will be seen as a high priority to resolve for healing and restoration in this nation's cities.

As Christians we should be on the forefront of this effort. Any seasoned Christian is familiar with the following passage of scripture:

> If my people, which are called by my name, shall humble themselves, and pray, and seek my face, and turn from their wicked ways; then will I hear from heaven, and will forgive their sin, and will heal their land. (II Chronicles 7:14)

Upon careful consideration of each phrase we see a step-by-step guide we could use to recover from racism. This passage illustrates the power of repentance and the blessings that could flow if we, God's people, follow these instructions. Let us therefore examine each phrase.

"If my people . .."

Who are God's people? God is talking to those of us who are His, who are the called according to His purpose. He is referring to those who walk with Him and talk with Him, in other words, those who have a relationship with Him. In this age, the age of grace, that would mean people who are saved—true Christians.

"Who are called by my name . .."

God's good name is at stake here. It is not about any of us. Christians should uphold His good name by being leaders in solving this matter. Because of the historical connection between slavery and Christianity, Christ's name has been besmirched. This is a great enough incentive for us to seek solutions.

"Would humble themselves. .."

Humility demands that white people get over their superiority complex. Humble prayer requires black people to give up self-serving pity and anger.

"and pray . .."

We should not try to organize, analyze, politicize or do anything without FIRST getting direction from God. He is the master of all things. Hearkening to His voice and His instruction is critical for success.

"And seek my face . .."

What is God's will concerning black and white people? What is His way—to the solution? How would He have us to go about getting free from this bondage? As we have learned from our valiant but limited human attempts, redressing the wrongs cannot happen before clearly acknowledging what the problem is. These things have to happen in the right order. This is where the waters got muddied after the Civil Rights movement. The laws ended up not addressing slavery and its descendents directly, but all who have been oppressed. This is not a bad thing, but it skirts the issue of the sin of racism.

"And turn from their wicked ways . .."

Stop all of our wicked, racist dogma. Stop stereotyping black and white people. Let us guard our tongues from promoting long accepted falsehoods. "White people are always thus and so." "Black people always do this and that." We have so many dogmatic assertions that have to be abandoned if we want a fresh anointing here. None of us knows every single white or black person therefore, we cannot speak for all of them. It starts with how we think, which influences how we speak, which in turn dictates our actions. Our speech patterns need scourging. There is life and death in the power of the tongue. (Proverbs 18:21) Our ill-willed thoughts and deeds should be abandoned. Our minds and hearts need changing.

"Then will I hear from heaven . . ."

All the noise and clamour of white supremacy and black self-righteousness is nothing but annoying noise to God. But our humble, sincere, petitions He will hear. He promised.

"And will forgive their sin . . ."

Isn't God good! He forgives our sins. He will forgive us of slavery, racism, and un-forgiveness.

"And will heal their land . . ."

(This just gets better and better!) God will actually heal us of racism, but we have to be willing and ready. Then, regardless of whether this nation ever confesses, repents, and redressing the wrongs, it will be out of our hands. We as Christians and we as black people will be empowered to let the bitterness go.

The third part of the spiritual healing process is the forgiveness piece. Volumes and volumes have been written about this in the Christian world. Preachers and teachers are never through with this subject. Why, because it is the cornerstone of Christian faith. And because we struggle so greatly to live it out. Let us therefore take a special look at forgiveness with regard to the sin of racism.

Christianity says that when Jesus Christ hung on the cross and died, He paid the price for sin. He took my and your place and endured the wrath of the Father for us for all the wrongs we have ever done and will ever do. It stands to reason then, that He paid the price for all of the wrongs that slave owners, slave drivers, and slave merchants did. Jesus paid the price for all the whippings, the rapes, the lynchings, castrations, fires, tearing away of babes from mothers, husbands from wives, and siblings from one another—and all the horrors of the Middle Passage. He hung on the cross to pay for all of the evil and inhumanity of slavery, all the unfairness of discrimination. Unfortunately, as black people, we are trying to bear the heavy load of racism on our own. We get so angry and upset over continued racial injustice. We carry around our hurt and pain. It is heavy, too heavy, in fact for mere humans. That is why we have heart disease, hypertension, and other stress-related diseases. Jesus said:

Come unto me all ye that labour and are heavy laden, and I will give you rest. (Matthew 11:28)

We cannot bear this burden ourselves. This battle is not ours. That is not to say that we do nothing. We should protest injustice, report racial incidences, and do whatever God calls us to do to bring about change. But we should not try to bear it spiritually by carrying this bitter burden around with us day and night. If racism colors all of your thoughts, actions, and decisions, you have gone too far. You have not given it over to Christ, trusting that He has handled it all.

But he was wounded for our transgressions, he was bruised for our iniquities; the chastisement of our peace was upon him; and with his stripes we are healed. (Isaiah 53:5)

If you are an angry black person because you feel justice has not been done, imagine this: Imagine all the revenge and punishment you would like to inflict on every white person who ever treated you cruelly or unjustly because of their racist hatred. Image the force of all the anger you have. Multiply that by all the anger of every black who has suffered—both living and dead. Now—imagine Jesus on the cross bearing all that punishment—*because that is what He did*!!!!!! He was wounded for the transgressions of mankind, not only those inflicted against you, but those you have inflicted on others. And actually the ones you have inflicted on others are more critical for you to focus on because it is our own sins that tear us apart from God. How can we be healed: *by His stripes.* Yes, by His stripes we are healed. *Jesus Christ is the cure all, end all, stop all, all in all!*

He will fix this problem and wash us clean, that is *IF* we humbly admit this sin of racism and ask for forgiveness.

Un-forgiveness is a spiritual killer. There are two aspects to remember here, un-forgiveness as in never asking for it (this nation) and un-forgiveness as in never granting it (black people). I, as well as many other descendants of slavery, have not forgiven white people and America for the enslavement of our ancestors and for now pretending like this is a bygone, long-long time-ago-in-a-far-away-place issue. I still get angry, I do admit, even though I have no right knowing how Christ has forgiven me of my every sin. Un-forgiveness is the thing that is stopping healing in black communities. I, like many black people, have been waiting for this nation to confess and repent and *ask for forgiveness* before I forgive. But that is not what Jesus did. He bore our sins, my sins, and forgave me before I ever confessed or repented. Therefore we (blacks) can be healed by admitting the hurt, anger and shame, laying it on the altar before God—and leaving it there.

> And when ye stand praying, forgive, if ye have ought against any: that your Father also which is in heaven may forgive you your trespasses. But if ye do not forgive, neither will your Father which is in heaven forgive your trespasses. (Matthew 11:25–26)

In this passage of scripture Jesus is not saying that the Father will withhold the ultimate forgiveness through salvation. Salvation is not of works, but by grace (Ephesians 2:8–9). You cannot lose your salvation once you are saved. But when we try to carry around our un-forgiveness, it strains our relationship with God. We lose our peace and miss out on blessings and freedom here

on earth. We lose focus of him and the peace and joy of His
great gift of forgiveness.

In his book *The Gift of Forgiveness*, Dr. Charles Stanley, a
renowned Christian pastor and evangelist describes un-
forgiveness as "a consuming corruption."

> The destructive nature of an unforgiving spirit is such that it is
> not limited to one relationship. Resentment and other negative
> feelings spill over into other relationships.[2]

He describes how one of the ways an unforgiving spirit can
destroy a life is through "the waiting game."

> Since the person with the unforgiving spirit is usually waiting
> for the other person to make restitution, a great deal of time
> may go by. During this time, fleshly patterns of behavior and
> incorrect thought processes develop. As I mentioned before,
> other relationships are damaged. Even after an unforgiving
> spirit is corrected, the side effects can take years to deal with,
> especially in the area of relationships.
>   The irony of the situation is this: By refusing to forgive
> and by waiting for restitution to be made, individuals allow
> their personal growth and development to hinge on the deci-
> sion of others they dislike to begin with.[3]

Just look at how disproportionately African Americans are
affected by dysfunctional relationships! It is our un-forgiveness
haunting us. We are waiting for racism to end before we can
have peace and happiness. No justice—no peace!

Dr. Stanley goes on to emphasize how "some choose to
lose."

> I hope you clearly understand this: A person who harbors un-
> forgiveness always loses. Regardless of how wrong the other
> person may have been, refusing to forgive means reaping cor-
> ruption in life. And that corruption begins in one relationship,
> including the relationship with God, and works its way into all
> the rest.
> Holding on to hurt is like grabbing a rattlesnake by the tail;
> you are going to be bitten. As the poison of bitterness works

its way through the many facets of your personality, death will occur—death that is more far-reaching than your physical death, for it has the potential to destroy those around you as well.[4]

Perhaps all this is beginning to make some spiritual sense to you, but you are still hindered by one aspect. You still want to get even. You want and eye for an eye as the Old Testament describes. If this is you, please ponder deeply this truth: *Vengeance* belongs to God. It is too poisonous for our human hearts, which were never meant to know good and evil, to handle. The bitterness of it spreads from one area of our lives to another like a cancer.

> Dearly beloved, avenge not yourselves, but rather give place unto wrath: for it **is** written, **Vengeance is mine**; I will repay, saith the Lord. (Romans 12:19)

God's anger is justified because He is completely holy and perfect. His judgments are right and pure therefore. Our anger on the other hand only begets more anger—and more sin, too! The following passages describe the dangers of angry living.

> An angry man stirreth up strife, and a furious man aboundeth in transgression. (Proverbs 29:22)

> Be not hasty in thy spirit to be angry: for anger resteth in the bosom of fools. (Ecclesiastes 7:9)

The sin of racism has now been compounded by the sin of un-forgiveness. Does this mean that the first sin has been nullified. No. God gets the final say. All racists and oppressors will have to answer to Him.

> For we must all appear before the judgment seat of Christ; that every one may receive the things done in his body, according to that he hath done, whether it be good or bad. (II Corinthians 5:10)

While we are involved in the process of healing from racism we should keep in mind that because it is a spiritual problem, we are doing spiritual battle. Most Christians are familiar with the passages in the Bible that pertain to warfare in the spiritual realm. Therefore, we know that our carnal weapons will not work against this enemy.

> For the weapons of our warfare are not carnal, but mighty through God to the pulling down of strongholds: (II Corinthians 10:4)

> For we wrestle not against flesh and blood, but against principalities, against powers, against the rulers of the darkness of this world, against spiritual wickedness in high places. (Ephesians 6:12)

We must adorn the full armour *of God*, as described in Ephesians, chapter 6, in order to win this war on a spiritual level.

> Stand therefore, having your loins girt about with truth, and having on the breastplate of righteousness: and your feet shod with the preparation of the gospel of peace; Above all, taking the shield of faith, wherewith ye shall be able to quench all the fiery darts of the wicked. And take the helmet of salvation, and the sword of the Spirit, which is the word of God. (Ephesians 6:14–17)

To have the truth wrapped around your waist like a belt means that you are always prepared to speak the truth about racism. You and I should not be afraid to speak up regardless of the people around or the circumstance. Stand therefore to say that racism is wrong, that it is a direct result of slavery, and that truthfully Jesus is the only cure.

What do we know to be right and righteous in our hearts? It is right to repent, apologize, forgive, and pay restitution. If that were done this nation could honestly don the breastplate of righteousness. She would then be protected from having this compounded sin thrown back into her face at every crisis. She could then say, no, you can no longer condemn me for racism. I did the right thing by way of my black citizens.

What does it mean to have feet shod with the preparation of the gospel of peace? We should be prepared for peace talks. We have to be willing to come together with the olive branch in hand. We should be resolved to go anyplace and do anything necessary to obtain peace. Jesus called the peacemakers blessed in His sermon on the mount (Matthew 5). Also, the gospel of peace is the good news of salvation through Christ, which, again should be our ultimate goal in all wars against injustice.

> Peace I leave with you, my peace I give unto you: not as the world giveth, give I unto you. Let not your heart be troubled, neither let it be afraid. (John 14:27)

Peace is our inheritance as Christians. Jesus gave it to us and we should not let the world take it away. We bandy about that word, "peace," so much so that now it has become hackneyed and devoid of meaning. But with the true peace, the peace of God, we can breath life back into it and into this seemingly hopeless situation. Let the Holy Spirit, not our own agendas, lead and guide us in the peace process.

During this battle it is critical to believe that God will win, that He has in fact already won. This faith will be the shield that blocks the fiery darts of negativism and pessimism that racism will never end. We also need to keep in mind the thing forgotten in many of the previous battles: salvation is more important than any earthly issue. Slavery and racism are finite earthly states. Salvation, or lack of it, is an eternal, irreversible state. What does it profit a black person to gain apologies, vengeance, restitutions, and more rights and laws and then lose his or her very soul upon death? To don the helmet of salvation is to protect our minds from letting other penetrating agendas get priority over salvation.

Finally, do not be afraid to use the Word of God, the Bible. It is the sword that cuts right to the heart of the enemy's ploys and exposes them for the lies that they are. Many Christians shy away from reading or quoting the word of God directly because they do not want to be labeled an extremist. But God's Word is the ultimate offensive weapon. It goes forth and does not return to Him void (Isaiah 55:11). Ground will be gained through knowing and spreading God's word. He is the creator of all things and so His perspective matters the most.

One practical step I recommend in fighting this spiritual battle is fellowship. I encourage it, especially among black and white Christians. We are the example to the world, God's representatives here on earth. Let us begin by visiting each other's churches, listening to one another's music, and socializing together at our homes and at church functions. We should also speak honestly to each other about racism, encouraging action, apology, and forgiveness all around. We should try understanding each other's history and culture. Black Christians may have a head start here being that our culture immersed within the larger society. We learn much of "white" history in schools and through current events. All these things, however, are somewhat abstract learning. When you talk with and become friends with a real live person, their experiences and perspective are more valuable.

Let us also pray without ceasing. Sometimes our prayers are too small. Let us ask for the seemingly impossible and expect a miracle! Ask God directly for racism to end, for healing to occur for individuals, the corporate body of Christ, and this nation as an entity. Let us pray for mercy, understanding, and compassion to come forth like rivers of water. But especially pray for salvation. Pray for the salvation of those who are being blinded from seeing the beauty of Christ by racial anger and frustration. Pray also for those blinded by their own sense of superiority. Pray for people's personal repentance and salvation. This could cause revival like this country has never seen. Racial peace and harmony might break out as a direct result of those people who are now hindered by racism being changed and coming to Christ in droves! Another artist I love sings these words, words I often pray concerning racism in America:

Believe the unbelievable.
Receive the inconceivable.
And see beyond our wildest imaginations.

Oh Lord, we come, with great expectations.[5]
"Great Expectations"
written and recorded by Steven Curtis Chapman*

I grew up in America during the Cold War era. Our country was stockpiling weapons of mass destruction and the Russians were racing to beat our efforts. It was referred to as the arms race. Many people were in despair over the futility of it all, because even a small fraction of these weapons, if deployed, would destroy the earth. Even though the leaders of these two superpowers would meet regularly to negotiate how to end this war, there was a gloomy sense of inevitable doom. People were sure this would be the end, Armageddon (as the secular world understands it). Then on December 8, 1991 came the shocking announcement from a group of former presidents of Russia that the U.S.S.R. "as a subject of international and geopolitical reality *no longer exists*. [emphasis mine]" Just like that. In one day people went from being sure the world would soon end by nuclear war between Russia and the United States to the U.S.S.R. becoming non-existent. Most people could not have even conceived of it the day before.

Another miraculous event preceded this one by about two years. A city that had been divided since 1961 suddenly became one again. The city of Berlin, Germany had been split in two due . to unresolved territory disputes from World War II. Family and friends had been literally torn apart as East Berliners were physically trapped by authorities in their half of the city in order to stop mass exodus to the democratic side of the world. For almost 30 years they did not see the other side because of the Iron Curtain, as the Berlin Wall was commonly known. Their situation seemed hopeless. Then one day in 1989, Hungary announced it was opening up the wall. This was a newsflash that spread worldwide like wildfire. People were happily shocked. Although the factors leading up to this historical occasion had been brew-

---

* The song "Great Expectations," written by Steven Curtis Chapman, © 1999 Peach Hill Songs 2/Sparrow Song. All Rights Reserved. Used by Permission.

ing beforehand, people had gotten used to the wall. They were probably resigned to despair thinking they would never see loved ones on the other side ever again. They thought the wall would never come down. But come down it did, and that almost in a day!

The fall of the system of Apartheid in South Africa is a similar saga. The racial oppression was so great that if you had told them in 1974 that not only would their strict system of racial segregation and oppression be abolished, but also that they would have a black president by 1994 you would have been laughed at by most. But that is exactly what happened!

Think now about the monumentality of the Middle Passage: millions and millions of people tortured beyond description to complete this horrific journey. Many more millions jumped or were thrown overboard whose bones are at the bottom of the sea. Think about the seemingly insurmountable specter of chattel slavery. Reducing a people to work as animals, generation after generation, century after century. Time has not been able to heal this hurt with wounds that are continuously picked raw. Think about the blood money that was made, the ill-gotten gain fueled by greed, and where it might be today. How about the fearsome and angry pride some still cling to in the name of "heritage" or "unity." Examining the confusion the enemy has wrought through so-called science boggles the mind and makes one want to holler and throw up their hands. Think of the deception and lies that have many knotted up in a ball of spiritual anger and blindness. What of the debilitating affect on the most power-filled group of people on the face of the earth—the Christian brotherhood? Now look in any low-income, poverty stricken, black neighborhood and see the despair and frustration. It is written all over the people's faces who stand on the streets and stare. The haunting hollowness of it protrudes from the depths of their eyes. It seems to have no end.

Now look to the future. Imagine people in the future looking back on this period of slavery and its legacy of racism as a dark spot of confusion and evil in the history of the world, a 500-year glitch so to speak. Imagine them marveling in disbelief and sadness that people actually thought in terms of races and treated people cruelly because of skin color and cultural features. Imagine it as a strange and unnatural divider that collapsed suddenly, as a war that did not seem to have any good end but suddenly ended, an oppressive weight suddenly lifted.

Pray and meditate on this question: Is anything too hard for the Lord? That is what He asked Sarah and Abraham in response to her disbelief that she, at ninety years old, could have a child with her husband who was 120. (Genesis 18:14) Not only did she have that child, but their descendants from that offspring were (are) as numerous as the stars in heaven—just as God had promised (Genesis 15:1–5). This is the same God who parted the Red Sea, the one who tumbled the walls of Jericho. He came here in the form of a man through a virgin birth. He ended the Cold War and toppled the Berlin Wall. He made Nelson Mandela president of South Africa. Is He able to purge us of our greed and pride concerning racism? Can He heal our anger and despair? Can He take the stars in His hand and count them? Can He number the sand on the sea shore. Yes, He can! Therefore, He can untangle this knotted mess. He can break the bonds of Satan's yoke of lies to bring people unto Himself. He can heal His own Body and cause us to be one as we ought. He is infinite and infinitely powerful.

He is able to move mountains.
He has empowered us to move mountains.
Mountains of anger.
Mountains of fear.
Mountains of covetousness, bitterness, doubt.
Centuries of lies and lying.
Yes. He is able.
Amen.

Chapter Seven Endnotes

1. There is the alternate argument that the Civil War was motivated more by economics than by moral initiative. I subscribed to this theory at one point. However, now I believe that it was a moral calling for many, especially for the black soldiers involved.

2. Stanley, Charles, *The Gift of Forgiveness Put the Past Behind You and Give . . .*, (Nashville, TN: Thomas Nelson, Inc., 1987) 5–6.

3. Stanley, *The Gift of Forgiveness*, 9–10.

4. Stanley, *The Gift of Forgiveness*, 11.

5. Steven Curtis Chapman, *"Great Expectations,"* Speechless, Sparrow Song/Peach Hill Songs, Brentwood, TN, 1999.

Bibliography

Beck, Sanderson. *Middle East and Africa to 1875*, quoted on the website www.san.beck.org/1-14-Africa1800-1875.html.

Bennett, Jr., Lerone. *Before the Mayflower: a History of Black America*. Chicago: Johnson Publishing Co., 1962 (updated "Landmarks and Milestones" section (New York: Penquin Books, 1993))

Cann, Rebecca L., Mark Stoneking, and Allen c. Wilson. "Mitochondrial DNA and Human Evolution," *Nature 325*. London: Nature Publishing Group, 1987.

Chapman, Steven Curtis. "Great Expectations," *Speechless*, compact disc. Brentwood, TN: Sparrow Records, 1999.

Curtin, Philip D. *Africa Remembered: Narratives by West Africans from the Era of the Slave Trade*. Prospect Heights, Il.: Waveland Press, Inc., 1997.

Core Lane, Jr. "The Catholic Church and Slavery." website http://ic.net/~erasmus/RAZ168.HTM. Lane Core, Jr., 1997, quoted on The Crime Prevention Group website. Leroy J. Pletten, 1999 http://medicolegal.tripod.com/catholicsvslavery.htm.

Crime Prevention Group, The, "Roman Catholic Church Opposition to Slavery," Leroy J. Pletten, 1999 on website http://medicolegal.tripod.com/catholicsvslavery.htm.

Equiano, Olaudah. *The Interesting Narrative of the Life of Olaudah Equiano, or Gustavus Vassa the African* (1789). quoted on Washington State University website http://www.wsu.edu:8000/~dee/Equiano.html.

Evangelical Press. "Bob Jones University Drops Interracial Dating Ban," *Christianity Today*. http://www.ctlibrary.com/15329. March 6, 2000.

Franklin, Kirk, "The Blood Song," *The Rebirth of Kirk Franklin*, compact disc. Englewood, CA: Gospocentric, 2002.

Harding, Vincent. *There is a River: The Struggle for Freedom in America.* New York: Harvest/HBT Book, reissue edition, 1993 quoted on The Mariners' Museum website, "Resistance and Endurance," *Captive Passage: The Transatlantic Slave Trade and the making of the Americas.* http://www.mariner.org/captivepassage/departure/dep015.html.

Ham, Ken, Carl Weiland, and Don Batten. *One Blood: The Biblical Answer to Racism.* Green Forest, AR: Master Books, Inc., 1999.

Harms, Robert. *The Diligent: a Voyage Through the Worlds of the Slave Trade.* New York: Basic Books, 2002.

Kacela, Rev. Xolani. "Do Good Christians Party," *Dallasblack.com.* *http://dallasblack.com/cgi-bin/main.pl?state=show_article&id=61.* Sept. 3, 2002.

Lewis, Clive Staples. *Mere Christianity.* New York: HarperCollins, 1952.

Linsey, Joel and Regie Hamm, "Gather at the River," recorded by Point of Grace, *Rarities and Remixes*, compact disc, Paragon Music Corp, 1994.

Merriam-Webster Inc., Merriam-Webster Online Dictionary, www.m-w.com. Springfield, MA: Merriam-Webster Inc., 2005.

Nelson, Truman, *Documents of Upheaval: Selections from William Lloyd Garrison's THE LIBERATOR, 1831–1865.* New York: Hill and Wang, 1966, xvii quoted in The Crime Prevention Group website "Abolitionists Opposing Slavery and Tobacco." 1998, 1999 http://medicolegal.tripod.com/abolitionists.htm#Garrison.

Nockels, Nathan and Tom Laune (producers). "America", recorded by Passion: *One Day Live*, compact disc. Six Steps Music, 2000.

Nye, Russel B., *William Lloyd Garrison and the Humanitarian Reformers.* Boston: Little, Brown and Co, 1955 quoted in The Crime Prevention Group website "Abolitionists Opposing Slavery and Tobacco." 1998, 1999 http://medicolegal.tripod.com/abolitionists.htm#Garrison.

Payne, Jennifer M., "Influences of British Imperialist Economic Fortunes on Slavery, Sugar, Abolition" The Wedderburn Pages website, 1994 http://wedderburn.alpesprovence.net/slavhist.htm

Powell, Mac, Samuel Tai Anderson, Brad Avery, David Carr, and Mark D. Lee "Come Together," *Come Together,* compact disc. New Spring Publishing, Inc/Vandura 2500 Songs, 2001.

Robert Appleton Company, "Early African Church," *The Catholic Encyclopedia, Vol. 1,* (1907) quoted on The Catholic Encyclopedia, online edition, (K. Knight, 2005), http://www.newadvent.org/cather/01191a.htm.

Robinson, Randall. *The Debt: What America Owes to Blacks.* New York: Penquin Putnam, 2000.

Shipman, Pat. *The Evolution of Racism: Human Differences and the Use and Abuse of Science.* New York: Simon and Schuster, 1994.

Snyder, Howard N., "Sexual Assault of Young Children as Reported to Law Enforcement: Victim, Incident, and Offender Characteristics," *NCJ182990.* National Center for Juvenile Justice, July, 2000.

Stampp, Kenneth. *The Peculiar Institution: Slavery in the Ante-Bellum South.* New York: Alfred A. Knofp, Inc., 1956.

Stanley, Charles. *The Gift of Forgiveness: Put the Past Behind You and Give . . .* Nashville: Thomas Nelson, Inc., 1987.

Strobel, Lee. *The Case for Faith: a Journalist Investigates the Toughest Objections to Christianity.* Grand Rapids, MI: Zondervan Publishing House, 2000.

Thomas, Hugh. *The Slave Trade: The Story of the Atlantic slave Trade: 1440-1870.* New York: Touchstone, 1997.

U.S. Department of Justice, Office of Justice Program, Bureau of Justice Statistics, "Personal Crimes of Violence, 2000."

Various Contributors. *Life Applications Study Bible.* Wheaton, IL. Tyndale House Publisher, 1988.

Vanderlugt, Herb. "Kill the Spider," *Our Daily Bread.* Grand Rapids, MI: RBC Ministries, April 17, 2002.

Warren, Rick. *The Purpose Driven Church: Growth without Compromising Your Message and Mission.* Grand Rapids, Michigan: Zondervan Publishing House, 1995.

Index

Author
Biographical Sketch

Selena M. Johnson was born and raised in Bridgeport, Connecticut, a town that within her short lifetime changed from being a predominantly white, economically stable city to a rundown, crime-laden place with a majority minority population. As a young child she was usually the only African American in her class. In high school she experienced the results of desegregation through busing. She went on to attend the very prestigious Massachusetts Institute of Technology where she received a bachelor's degree in architecture. Then she matriculated to the University of California at Berkeley and obtained a Master of Architecture degree. During these years she realized how little she had been taught of her own culture. She began to study black history and culture and get involved with black activism.

She came to faith in Christ in the late 1990's after having been in membership at various churches throughout her life. Ames United Methodist Church in Maryland is her current church home. There she is actively involved in various ministries and is a certified lay speaker. Selena is also a wife and mother of one.

* 9 7 8 0 7 6 1 8 3 5 0 9 7 *